Margaretenspitze
Designs for Jewelry

Natural Forms in Macramé

by

Joan R. Babcock

Graphics by Jeff Babcock

Copyright © 2018, Joan R. Babcock

All rights reserved. No part of this book may be reproduced or transmitted in any form without permission from the author.

ISBN 978-0-9773052-4-7

Published by:
    Joan Babcock Designs
    16 Camerada Rd.
    Santa Fe, NM, 87508-8766
    www.joanbabcock.com
    www.micro-macramejewelry.com

First Printing - August 2018

Other works by Joan Babcock:

Micro-Macramé Jewelry: Tips and Techniques for Knotting with Beads
Wired Micro-Macramé Jewelry: Enhancing Fiber Designs with Wire
Micro-Macramé Jewelry II: Artful Designs for the Adventurous Knotter
Micro-Macramé and Cavandoli Knotting (DVD)

Even when tied in a thousand knots, the string is still but one.
    - Rumi

Table of Contents

Introduction   4

Materials and Tools   5

Technique Tips   5

Knot Diagrams   7

Projects

Project One - Dragonfly Earrings   9

Project Two - Dragonfly Pin   13

Project Three - Tropical Leaf Bracelet   18

Project Four - Oleander Earrings   24

Project Five - Oleander Bracelet   29

Project Six - Vine Bracelet   34

Project Seven - Margarete Swan Pin   39

Project Eight - Tulip Earrings   45

Project Nine - Zinnia Flower Necklace   50

Project Ten - Swallowtail Butterfly Pin   56

Project Eleven - Lunaria Bracelet   63

Project Twelve - Phoenix Necklace   70

Project Thirteen - Sunflower Bracelet, Pin, or Pendant   77

    Twisted Rope Pendant Chain   87

A Graceful Style of Knotting

When I first saw examples of Margaretenspitze a few years ago, I was captivated and delighted by it's beauty. This was a style of knotwork that reminded me of delicate lace with lyrical lines and patterns. With further research I learned that the technique was originated in Germany in the early 1900s by Margarete Naumann (1881-1946) who sought to create a knotting technique that was free of rigid structures. Her ideas are exemplified in the free-flowing look and curvilinear forms that characterize many Margaretenspitze designs. It is believed that Ms. Naumann died without leaving printed instructions, but fortunately, some of her pieces survived and have inspired others to continue in her footsteps.

So what is it that sets Margaretenspitze apart from other knotwork? A hybrid of macramé and knotted lace, Margaretenspitze has a particular style with a unique look and characteristics. It's fluid nature lends itself well to making open-work designs and floral motifs, so natural forms such as plants and flowers are a frequent subject. Beads are usually kept to a minimum, allowing the intricate knotwork itself to take center stage. Margaretenspitze designs are typically created with Half Hitch knots and variations such as the Double and Triple Half Hitches. A recurring theme within the knotwork is the gathering of cords into bundles (a.k.a. ropes or chains) and then the dispersing of cords from these bundles to facilitate new patterns.

In recent years there has been a growing interest in this fascinating technique. Books by Lotte Heinemann and Adriana Lazzari and other talented teachers have done much to advance the knowledge of this craft. Having created and taught micro-macramé jewelry myself for many years, I've worked in many different creative styles using knots and cord. But exploring the possibilities of Margaretenspitze has been a unique challenge that has given me much pleasure and reinvigorated my love of knotting. This book is the result of hundreds of hours of experimentation and trial and error. I've tried to stay true to the spirit of Margaretenspitze, using many of the universal elements, while developing my own interpretations. It is my hope that this book will contribute another look into the limitless potential of this lovely technique and encourage other knotters to create and explore.

Happy Knotting!

Joan

Materials and Tools

Figure 1

1. Nylon Cord (standard size #18) - This is the medium width (0.5mm) of S-Lon and C-Lon (see Fig. 1). Other #18 nylons such as Conso and Mastex can be used as well. **Note** - All of the projects in this book were specifically designed for this kind of cord. Other types and sizes of cord have not been tested with these projects and may not be suitable.

2. Macramé Knotting Board - I use either the 11" x 17" Macramé Project Board (see Fig. 2) or the 11.5" x 15.5" Beadsmith foam board. You can use whatever surface you prefer as long as it holds your pins securely.

3. Sewing or Quilting Pins - (Fig. 3a) I recommend that you keep your knotwork securely pinned down to the board. It will make the knotting process a lot easier and produce a better looking result. Rotate your piece as often as necessary so that you always have a comfortable angle for knotting.

4. Embroidery Scissors - (Fig. 3c) A pair of small sharp scissors are essential. Large or dull scissors can't fit into tight areas and won't cut the cords off closely and cleanly.

5. Embroidery and Sewing Needles - (Fig. 3b) You'll need a narrow embroidery needle such as a size #2 Crewel. I also like "Sharps", which have a smaller rounded eye. A medium size sewing needle will also be needed for finishing work and adding beads.

6. Thimble & Needle Nose Pliers - (see "Sewing Through Knotwork" in Technique Tips).

7. Clear Nail Polish - A small amount is applied to finishing knots (usually at the back of a piece) to prevent them from coming undone. Be careful not to apply too much because it can seep through the knotwork and darken the cord.

8. Beads & Findings - You can substitute beads of your own choosing for the beads that I've used in a project, as long as they are the same size and have large enough holes for the cord(s). See each project's title page for a suggested list of beads & findings.

Figure 2

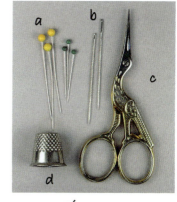

Figure 3

Conversion Chart - Inches to Millimeters

1/8" = 3.175mm, 1/4" = 6.35mm, 1/2" = 12.7mm, 3/4" = 19.05mm, 1" = 25.4mm

Technique Tips

1. Sewing through knotwork - To hide leftover cords or when adding beads, it may be necessary to sew the cord through existing knotwork. Depending on how dense the knotwork is, it can be difficult to pull the needle through. Here are some tips:

• Use a thimble (Fig. 3d) to help you to push the embroidery needle through the knotwork. Likewise, a pair of needle nose (or chain nose) pliers can help to pull the needle through tight spaces (see next tip).

• Once you get the needle into the knotwork, push it most of the way through. Grasp the eye-end of the needle and the knotwork between your thumb and first finger (see Fig. 4a), then rock the needle from side to side (see Fig. 4b) while pulling it through with your fingers or the pliers. This "rocking" method helps to ease the needle through without distorting the knotwork.

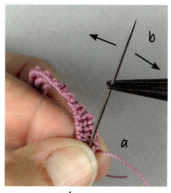

Figure 4

Joan Babcock

Materials and Tools, Technique Tips

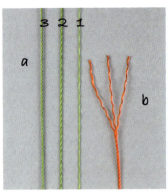

Figure 5

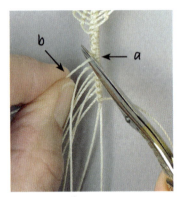

Figure 6

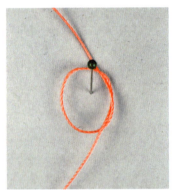

Figure 7

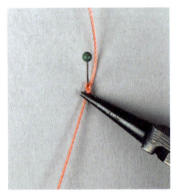

Figure 8

2. Ply reduction - #18 Nylon cords have three threads, otherwise known as "plies", that are twisted together. In some circumstances it's desirable to reduce the number of plies from 3-ply to 2-ply or 1-ply (see Fig. 5a). Ply reduction is usually done at the finishing stage of a piece and I use it often in this book.

• To divide a cord into 3 separate plies (see Fig. 5b), twist the cord to the right until the threads start to separate, then pull the threads apart. Use the blunt end of a sewing needle to get between the threads if needed.

• Finishing Work - There are often leftover cords at the end of a piece of knotwork that need to be eliminated. Reducing these cords to one or two plies makes them less bulky and easier to deal with. When a finishing knot such as an Overhand Knot is called for, reducing the plies in the cord or cords will make a smaller and less noticeable knot.

• Sewing Thread - You can use a single ply as an alternative to sewing thread. Although not as durable as authentic sewing thread, it's handy if you need an exact color to match your knotting cord. Passing it through beeswax will strengthen it.

3. Cutting off discarded cords - In most cases, the discarded cord should be cut off as close to the knotwork as possible so that it doesn't leave a visible nub. To do this, first stabilize the piece by pinning it to the board. Place the scissors tips around the cord that's going to be cut off (see Fig. 6a). The scissor blades should be almost closed, encircling the cord without cutting it. Push the scissors flush against the knotwork while pulling the cord outward (see Fig. 6b), then cut the cord.

4. Marking Cords - In most patterns, some of the cords will need to be eliminated as you progress through the pattern. To mark selected cords for elimination (or to spare them from elimination), make **OVK**s or use a magic marker at the tip of the cord(s).

5. Tightening Overhand Knots - Form the **OVK** but keep it loose. Place a narrow pin in the knotwork inside the **OVK** loop at the spot where you want it to tighten up (see Fig. 7). Slowly pull up the slack and tighten the knot around the pin. **Note** - Stop here and make sure that the knot is where you want it. It's easier to take it out when it's still semi-loose! Next, before removing the pin, grasp the cord just below the knot with needle nose pliers (see Fig. 8). Remove the pin. Push upwards towards the knot with the pliers while pulling outwards on the cord. Finish with a dab of clear nail polish to prevent the knot from coming undone.

Knots, Terms, and Abbreviations

KC - Knotting Cord : The active cord that wraps around another (anchor) cord.

AC - Anchor Cord : The stationary cord which holds the Knotting Cord.

LHK - Lark's Head Knot : This is used to attach (hitch) a new cord onto an Anchor Cord.

MH - Mounting Hitch : This is a Lark's Head Knot with the smooth side facing to the front and the bar to the back.

MTK - Mounting Knot : A **MH** with a **HH** added to each side to increase the width.

HH - Half Hitch : A single closed loop around an **AC**.

DHH - Double Half Hitch (AC in horizontal or diagonal position) : Two side by side **HH**s using the same cord. They are made in a Right to Left or Left to Right direction depending on the pattern. A **Triple Half Hitch (THH)** has three **HH**s.

VHH - Vertical Half Hitch : A **HH** with the **AC** in a vertical position.

R.VHH (or R.HH) : **KC** exits to the right.

L.VHH (or L.HH) : **KC** exits to the left.

VDHH - Vertical Double Half Hitch : A **DHH** with the **AC** in a vertical position.

R.VDHH - **KC** exits to the right.

L.VDHH - **KC** exits to the left.

VLHK - Vertical Lark's Head Knot : A **LHK** with a vertical **AC**. A series of **VLHK**s creates a **VLHK chain**, usually with the "spine" to the side.

HHch - Half Hitch Chain : A series of **HH**s (usually on a vertical **AC**) alternating between **R.VHH**s and **L.VHH**s. The **KC** is passed to the back of the chain between each **VHH**, which keeps the spine at the back of the chain.

AHHch - Alternating Half Hitch Chain : A chain of **HH**s in which each cord alternates being the **AC**.

FSQK - Flat Square Knot : see diagram.

OVK - Overhand Knot : see diagram.

Additional Terms

- **Lateral cords** - Horizontal cords which exit to the side(s) of a vertical row or bundle.
- **Bundle** - a group of cords wrapped together into a single unit by another cord or cords. Bundles can be short or long, thick or thin.
- **Row** - a horizontal or vertical line of knots (usually **DHH**s). **Note** - a row can be called a bundle when it has several **AC**s.
- **Chain** - A linear rope made of **HH**s that's often set apart from the rest of the knotwork.
- **Thread-Bar** - Random cords (or their fibers) located at the back side of the knotwork. When finishing a piece, leftover cords can be secured by sewing them under "thread-bars".

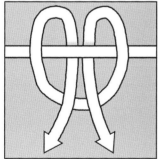
Mounting Hitch — Step 1 MH

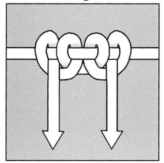
Mounting Knot — Step 2 MHK

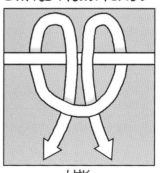
Larks Head Knot — LHK

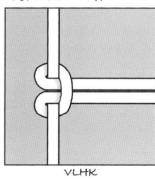
Vertical LHK — VLHK

Knots and Terms

Half Hitch (HH) & Double Half Hitch (DHH)

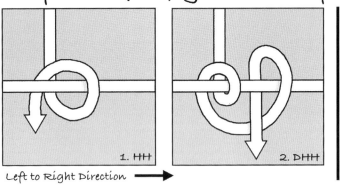
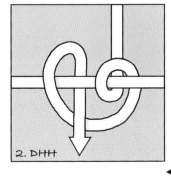
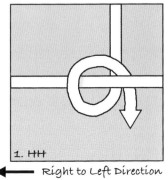

1. HH 2. DHH | 2. DHH 1. HH

Left to Right Direction →   ← Right to Left Direction

Vertical Half Hitch (VHH) & Vertical Double Half Hitch (VDHH)

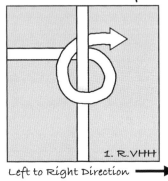
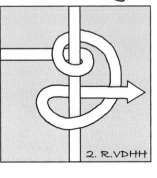
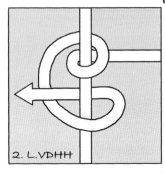
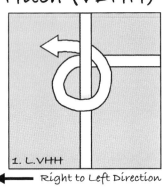

1. R.VHH 2. R.VDHH | 2. L.VDHH 1. L.VHH

Left to Right Direction →   ← Right to Left Direction

Half Hitch Chain (HHch) Alternate steps 1 and 2

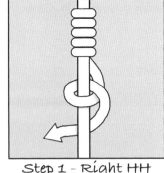
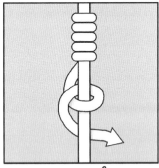
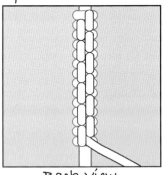
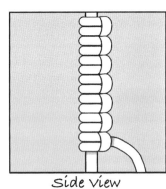

Step 1 - Right HH   Step 2 - Left HH   Back View   Side View

Alternating Half Hitch Chain (AHHch)   Overhand Knot   Flat Square Knot

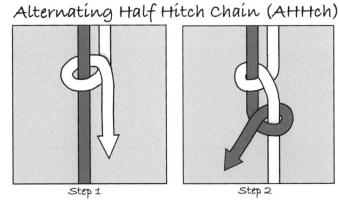
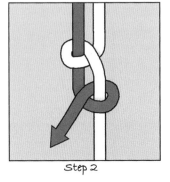
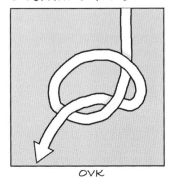

Step 1   Step 2   OVK   FSQK

8 Margaretenspitze Designs for Jewelry

Dragonfly Earrings

Materials

18g. Nylon Cord: Each earring requires 1 @ 30", 1 @ 60"
Findings: Fishhook ear wires
Beads: (2) 6° seed beads or any similar bead (must have a large enough hole to fit 4 cords) for the top/center.
Wing Beads: I used 7mm teardrops, 4mm fire polish, 8° and 10° seed beads, but you can use any small beads you prefer as long as they fit.
Embroidery Needle (narrow, #2 or similar)
Clear Nail Polish (optional but recommended)

Project One

Figure 1

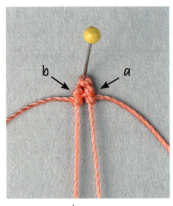
Figure 2

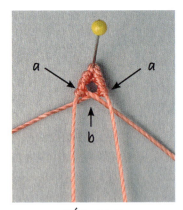
Figure 3

Dragonfly Body

1. Make an **OVK** at the center point of the 30" cord. Pin the **OVK** to your board and bring the two 15" cords downward. These will be the **AC**s (Anchor Cords) (see Fig. 1).

2. Center the 60" cord (the **KC**, Knotting Cord) behind the **AC**s and pin it in place temporarily. There should be 30" to the right and left of the center. With the right half of the **KC**, make an outward facing **VDHH** (Vertical Double Half Hitch) around the right-hand **AC** (see Fig. 2a). With the left half of the **KC**, make an outward facing **VDHH** around the left-hand **AC** (see Fig. 2b).

3. On each side, bring the **KC** back towards the center under the **AC** and make an inward facing **VDHH** (see Fig. 3a).

4. Cross the **KC**s at the center and bring them under the **AC** on the opposite side (see Fig. 3b). Make outward **VDHH**s (see Fig. 4).

5. Repeat Steps #3 & 4 five more times (see Fig. 5).

Small Wings

6. Reposition the body horizontally with the end to the right. Place a pin (see Fig. 6a) below the lower **AC** where it exits the **VDHH** and bring the **AC** downward vertically (see Fig. 6b). Use the lower **KC** (see Fig. 6c) to make a **Half Hitch chain** of 27 **HH**s (see Fig. 7). **Note -** To start the chain, bring the **KC** under the **AC** and to the left so that the cord exits to the left after the first **HH** of the chain.

7. After completing the chain, thread the **KC** onto an embroidery needle. Remove the pin from the start of the chain (Fig. 6a) and sew the **KC** through that same space (see Fig. 8a).

Figure 4

Figure 5

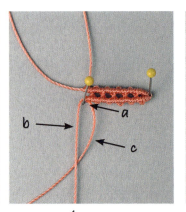
Figure 6

Figure 7

Margaretenspitze Designs for Jewelry

Dragonfly Earrings

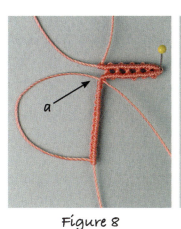
Figure 8

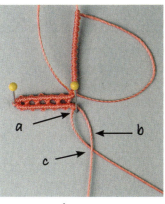
Figure 9

Figure 10

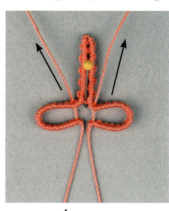
Figure 11

8. Reposition the body horizontally with the end to the left. Place a pin (see Fig. 9a) below the lower **AC** where it exits the **VDHH** and bring the **AC** downward vertically (see Fig. 9b). Use the lower **KC** to make a chain of 27 **HH**s. **Note -** To start the chain, bring the **KC** under the **AC** and to the right (see Fig. 9c) so that the cord exits to the right after the first **HH** of the chain.

9. After completing the chain, thread the **KC** onto an embroidery needle. Remove the pin from the start of the chain (Fig. 9a) and sew the **KC** through that same space (see Fig. 10). On each side, pull the **KC** through until the chain's beginning and ending come together forming loops which will be the lower wings (see Fig. 11).

10. Position the piece with the end up as in Figure 12. Pin the wings in place at the outer edges. Bring the **KC**s downward behind the piece at the center, crossing them to the opposite sides behind the **AC**s (see Fig. 12a). Make outward facing **VDHH**s on each side (see Fig. 13a).

Large Wings

- **Note -** The upper wings are made in the same way as the lower wings, but the **HH** chains will be longer. For Steps 11 - 14, refer to Figures 6 - 10.

11. Reposition the body horizontally with the end to the right. Place a pin below the lower **AC** where it exits the **VDHH** and bring the **AC** downward vertically. Use the lower **KC** to make a chain of 39 **HH**s. **Note -** Bring the **KC** under the **AC** and to the left so that the cord exits to the left after the first **HH** of the chain.

12. After completing the chain, thread the **KC** onto an embroidery needle. Remove the pin from the start of the chain and sew the **KC** through that same space.

13. Reposition the body horizontally with the end to the left. Place a pin below the lower **AC** where it exits the **VDHH** and bring the **AC** downward vertically. Use the lower **KC** to make a chain of 39 **HH**s. **Note -** Bring the **KC** under the **AC** and to the right so that the cord exits to the right after the first **HH** of the chain.

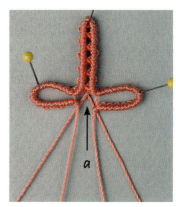
Figure 12

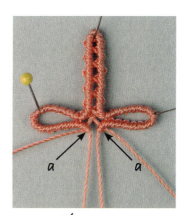
Figure 13

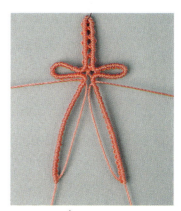
Figure 14

Joan Babcock

Project One

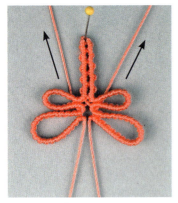

Figure 15

Figure 16

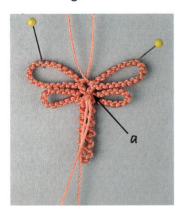

Figure 17

14. After completing the chain, thread the **KC** onto an embroidery needle. Remove the pin from the start of the chain and sew the **KC** through that same space. Figure 14 shows the completed chains with **KC**s sewn through. On each side, pull the **KC** completely through until the chain's beginning and end come together forming loops which will be the upper wings (see Fig. 15).

15. Flip the piece to the back and position it as in Fig. 16 with the **KC**s facing downward and the **AC**s facing upward. Bring the **KC**s together at the center/back and make a tight **OVK** (Overhand Knot), joining the cords together (see Fig. 17a).

Adding the Earring Wire

16. Thread the 2 **AC**s upward through the bead (see Fig. 18a). Thread the right-hand cord through the earwire loop in a right to left direction (see Fig. 18b). Thread the left-hand cord through the earwire loop in a left to right direction (see Fig. 18c).

17. Thread both cords downward through the bead (see Fig. 19) and tighten (see Fig. 20). Bring the cords to the back of the piece and make an **OVK** with both cords at the base of the bead (see Fig. 21a).

18. Apply a tiny dab of clear nail polish to both of the **OVK**s at the back and let dry (see Fig. 21). Cut off the excess cords close to the **OVK**s (not shown).

19. Optional - Sew beads into the interior of the wings for embellishment.

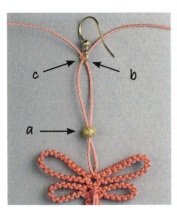

Figure 18

Figure 19

Figure 20

Figure 21

Dragonfly Pin or Pendant

Materials

18g. Nylon Cord: 2 @ 30", 1 @ 100"
Embroidery Needle
Sewing/beading Needle
Pin Option: ¾" to 1" Pin-back finding. Note - I prefer the narrow "solder-on" type, but you can use the wider type if preferred.
Pendant Option: 8 - 10mm jump ring or soldered ring
Beads: (1) 6 or 8mm round bead for the head. For the wings you can use any small beads that you prefer as long as they fit. For example, I used 6mm rounds, 3mm rondelles, 4mm rounds and bicones, 2mm spacers, 7mm teardrops, and 8° and 10° seed beads.

Project Two

Dragonfly Body

1. Line up the two 30" cords so the ends are even and make an **OVK** (Overhand Knot) at the center point of the cords, joining the cords. Pin the **OVK** to your board and bring the four 15" cords downward. These will be the **AC**s (Anchor Cords) (see Fig. 1).

Note - The body will consist of 2 parallel knotted chains with a space between them (see Fig. 5). If you are making the Pin version, make sure to leave enough space between the chains so that the knotwork is wide enough to conceal the Pin Back.

2. Center the 100" cord (the **KC**, Knotting Cord) behind the **AC**s and pin it in place temporarily. There should be 50" to the right and left of the center. With the right half of the **KC**, make an outward facing **VDHH** (Vertical Double Half Hitch) around the right-hand **AC**s. With the left half of the **KC**, make an outward facing **VDHH** around the left-hand **AC**s (see Fig. 2).

3. On each side, bring the **KC** towards the center under the 2 **AC**s and make an inward facing **VDHH** (see Fig. 3a).

4. Cross the **KC**s at the center and bring them under the **AC**s on the opposite side (see Fig. 3b). On each side, make an outward **VDHH** (see Fig. 4).

5. Repeat Steps #3 & 4 seven more times (see Fig. 5).

Small Wings

6. Reposition the body horizontally with the end to the right. Take one of the 2 lower **AC**s and bring it downward vertically. Use the lower **KC** to make a chain of 45 **HH**s (Half Hitches) (see Fig. 7). **Note** - To start the chain, bring the **KC** under the **AC** and to the left so that the cord exits to the left after the first **HH** of the chain (see Fig. 6).

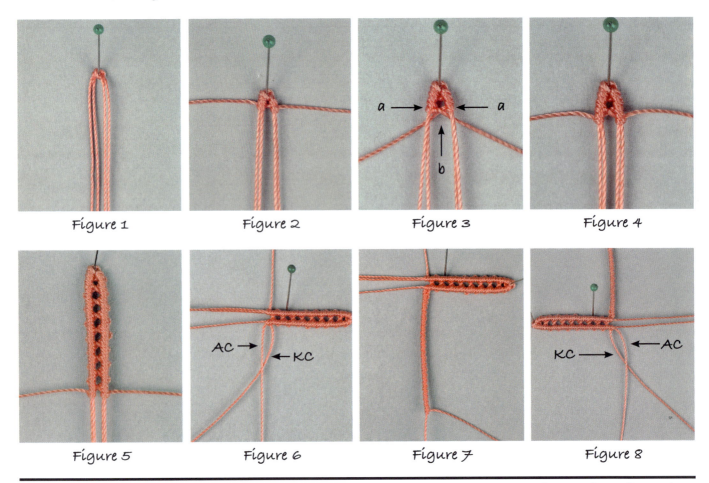

Figure 1 Figure 2 Figure 3 Figure 4

Figure 5 Figure 6 Figure 7 Figure 8

Margaretenspitze Designs for Jewelry

Dragonfly Pin

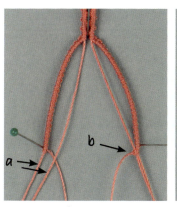
Figure 9

Figure 10

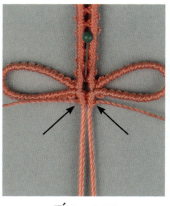
Figure 11

Figure 12

7. Reposition the body horizontally with the end to the left. Take one of the lower **AC**s and bring it downward vertically. Use the lower **KC** to make a chain of 45 **HH**s. **Note -** To start the chain, bring the **KC** under the **AC** and to the right so that the cord exits to the right after the first **HH** of the chain (see Fig. 8).

8. Reposition the body vertically and pin the ends of the **HH** chains to hold them in place. On each side, bring the loose **AC** parallel to the chain **AC** (see Fig. 9a). Make a tight inward facing **VDHH** around both **AC**s to join them (see Fig. 9b).

9. On each side, slide the **VDHH** upward on the loose **AC** until the chain end aligns with the chain start (see Fig. 10).

10. Pin both sides in place bringing the 2 **VDHH**s closely together. Cross the **KC**s to the opposite sides and make outward **VDHH**s (see Fig. 11).

11. Repeat Steps #3 & 4 (see Fig. 12).

Large Wings

Note - The large wings are made in the same way as the small wings, the only difference being that the chains are longer. Refer to Figures 6 - 8 if needed.

Figure 13

12. Reposition the body horizontally with the end to the right. Take one of the lower **AC**s and bring it downward vertically. Use the lower **KC** to make a chain of 69 **HH**s. **Note -** The cord should exit to the left after the first **HH** of the chain.

13. Reposition the body horizontally with the end to the left. Take one of the lower **AC**s and bring it downward vertically. Use the lower **KC** to make a chain of 69 **HH**s. **Note -** The cord should exit to the right after the first **HH** of the chain.

14. Reposition the body vertically and pin the ends of the **HH** chains to hold them in place. Make an **OVK** at the tip of each **HH** chain **AC** to mark it. On each side, bring the loose **AC** parallel to the **HH** chain **AC**. Make a tight inward facing **VDHH** around both **AC**s to join them (see Fig. 13).

15. On each side, slide the **VDHH** upward on the loose **AC** until the chain end aligns with the chain start. Retighten the **VDHH**s if necessary. Bring the **KC**s to the back of the piece (see Fig. 14).

Figure 14

Joan Babcock

Project Two

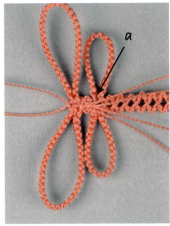

Figure 15

Head

16. Flip the piece to the back and, one at a time, sew each **KC** under the crossed cord that's located at the center back between the upper and lower wings. Pull through. Sew both loose **AC**s (not the **OVK AC**s) under the same crossed cord at the center back and pull through (see Fig. 15a).

17. Position the piece with the end up. Cut off the **OVK**s on the ends of the 2 hanging cords. Thread the head bead onto these cords and push it close to the wings (see Fig. 16a). **Note -** if you're making the pin, skip Step 18 and go on to Step 19.

18. Thread an 8mm soldered jump ring onto one of the cords (see Fig. 16b). Make a **Half SQK** (Half Square Knot - this is a single "over/under" knot) to capture the jump ring and pull it next to the bead (see Fig. 17).

19. Do the following with each cord: Thread it onto a needle. Pass the needle from front to back through the center space at the top of the knotwork between the wings (see Fig. 18a). Pull the cord through most of the way, leaving some loose cord out to the side of the bead. Bring the needle out to the front and pass it over the side cord (see Fig. 18b).

20. Tighten both cords around the bead by pulling them outwards (see Fig. 19). Flip the piece to the back and make a tight **Flat SQK** at the base of the bead (see Fig. 20).

Wing Beads

• When choosing beads to decorate the interior of the wings, use small beads (from seed beads to 6mm) and lay them within the wings to see how they fit and work together.

Tip - Sewing through knotwork can be made a lot easier with the help of these two tools: a thimble (to push the needle through) and a pair of needle nose pliers (to pull the needle through).

21. Untwist the **Flat SQK** cords and separate out a 1-ply thread from each cord (see Fig. 21a). Sew the 2-ply segments under the crossed cord at the center back (see Fig. 21b).

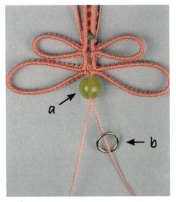

Figure 16

Figure 17

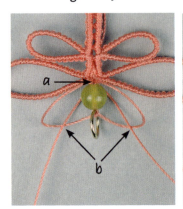

Figure 18

Figure 19

Figure 20

Figure 21

Margaretenspitze Designs for Jewelry

Dragonfly Pin

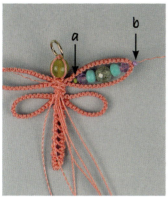
Figure 22

Figure 23

Figure 24

Figure 25

22. Starting on either side: Thread the 1-ply thread onto a sewing or beading needle. On the inside "V" of the wing, sew under one or two cords in the **HH** chain to move the thread outward a tiny bit (about 1mm from the "V" in the wing) and bring the needle out (see Fig. 22a). Thread the beads onto the needle and check that they fit within the length of the wing (I recommend that you use a seed bead at the start of the strand because it will fit better within the wing). At the outside tip of the wing, sew through the chain to the outside (see Fig. 22b).

23. Thread on a seed bead and sew back through the chain (bypassing the seed bead) and through all of the beads. Sew under one or two cords in the opposite **HH** chain from where the thread entered the wing (see Fig. 23 for Steps 23 - 26).

24. Bring the thread out at the back of the piece. To secure the group of loose cords at the back of the piece, sew around them several times and tie them down securely to the dragonfly body.

25. Use the same thread (if it's too short, take a 1-ply thread from another loose cord at the back) to sew the beads into the lower wing on the same side, following the same method as in the upper wing. Secure the thread at the center by sewing back and forth through the grouped cords a few times and cut it off.

26. Using the 1-ply thread from the opposite side, sew in the beads for the remaining wings. If making the pendant, cut off all of the grouped cords just below the lower wings. If making the pin, see Step #27.

Finishing

27. Pin Option - Separate a 1-ply cord from one of the grouped cords to use as thread for attaching the pin backing. Cut off all of the other grouped cords just below the lower wings. Sew the pin backing to the back of the dragonfly body.

28. Antennae for Pin (optional) - Thread a 10" piece of cord onto an embroidery needle and pass one end (back to front) under the right side cord that surrounds the "head" bead (see Fig. 24a). Pass the other end (back to front) under the left side cord (see Fig. 24b). Pass both ends through the center loop (Fig. 24c) of the 10" cord and pull taut. On each cord, add as many seed beads as you wish (I used an 11° seed bead, an 8° bead, then another 11° bead). Make a tight **OVK**. Add a dab of clear nail polish, let dry and cut off the excess cord (see Fig. 25).

29. Pendant Option - Use a finished chain or make the Twisted Rope Chain from this book.
Important - thread the Twisted Rope Chain through the top ring of the Dragonfly before attaching the clasp to the chain or it won't fit.

Tropical Leaf Bracelet

Materials

14 cords @ 44"
(2) 6 - 8mm jump rings
(1) Magnetic clasp

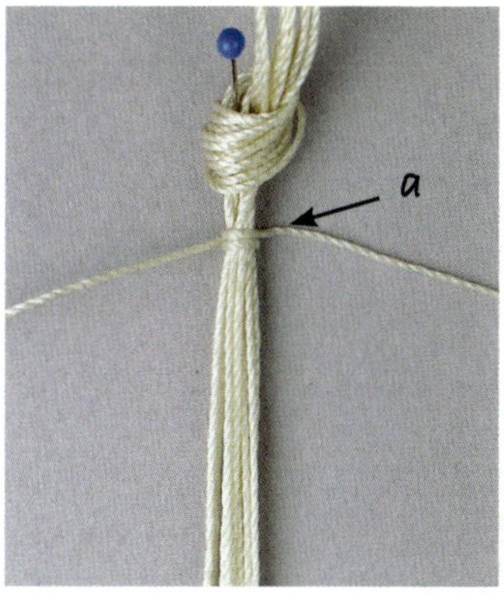

Tropical Leaf Bracelet

Part 1 - Bracelet, Right Half

Leftward Leaf

1. Bundle together 13 cords so that the ends are even. Temporarily tie the cords together with an **OVK** (Overhand Knot) at the center point (22" from the end) of the cords (see Fig. 1). Pin the **OVK** to the board with the cords positioned vertically. Below the **OVK**, attach the remaining cord tightly around the bundle (see Fig. 1a) with a **VDHH** (Vertical Double Half Hitch).

2. With the right-hand **VDHH** cord, make a **L.HH** (Half Hitch with the cord exiting to the left), then a **R.HH** (Half Hitch with the cord exiting to the right). Leave this lateral cord to the right side of the bundle (see Fig. 2a). The left half of the **VDHH** cord (Fig. 2b) will not be used until Part 2 of the bracelet.

3. Take a new cord from the back center of the bundle and make a **R.VDHH** (Vertical Double Half Hitch with the cord exiting to the right). Leave this lateral cord to the right side of the bundle (see Fig. 2).

4. Repeat step 3 until there are 13 lateral cords to the right of the bundle. There should be only one vertical **AC** (Anchor Cord) remaining (see Fig. 2).

5. Thread an embroidery needle onto the **AC**. Flip the piece over and locate the 3rd lateral cord from the top. Sew through (from right to left) the thread bars at the base of this 3rd cord (see Fig. 3) and pull the **AC** through so that the narrow bundle end is next to the upper bundle, forming a loop (see Fig. 4). **Note** - the needle may cause the upper bundle cord(s) to loosen. Retighten them if necessary.

6. Flip the piece to the front again and bring the **AC** out to the left (see Fig. 4a). It will now function as a **KC** (Knotting Cord). Pin the piece so that the loop stays tightly in place. Bring the **KC** downward under the topmost lateral cord on the left and make a **DHH** (Double Half Hitch) around it. Continue bringing the **KC** downward and make **DHH**s around the next 4 lateral cords (see Fig. 5).

7. On the right side, take the topmost lateral cord and use it as a **KC**. Bring it down under the 2nd lateral cord and make a **DHH**. Continue bringing the **KC** downward and make **DHH**s around the next 5 lateral cords (see Fig. 6).

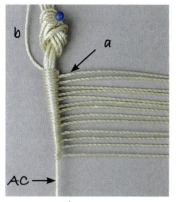

Figure 1

Figure 2

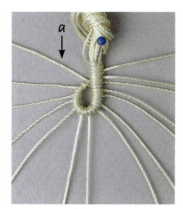

Figure 3

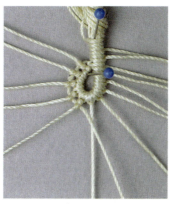

Figure 4

Figure 5

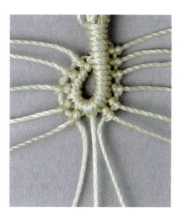

Figure 6

Joan Babcock

Project Three

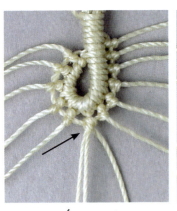
Figure 7

Figure 8

Figure 9

Figure 10

8. There should be one unknotted vertical cord at the bottom of the loop. Align the right-hand **KC** with this cord. Bring the left-hand **KC** to the right under both cords and make a **VDHH** around the 2 cords (see Fig. 7). This is the start of a center bundle in which all of the cords will be gathered.

9. On the left side, bring the topmost cord downward and using it as a **KC**, make **DHH**s around the next 4 lateral cords. On the right side, bring the topmost cord downward and using it as a **KC**, make **DHH**s around the next 5 lateral cords (see Fig. 8).

10. Align the right-hand **KC** with the 3 center bundle cords. Bring the left-hand **KC** to the right under the 4 cords and make a **VDHH** around the cords (see Fig. 8, center).

11. On the left side, bring the topmost cord downward and using it as a **KC**, make **DHH**s around the next 3 lateral cords. On the right side, bring the topmost cord downward and using it as a **KC**, make **DHH**s around the next 4 lateral cords (see Fig. 9 for Steps 11 & 12).

12. Align the right-hand **KC** with the 5 center bundle cords. Bring the left-hand **KC** to the right under the 6 cords and make a **VDHH** around the cords.

13. On the left side, bring the topmost cord downward and using it as a **KC**, make **DHH**s around the next 2 lateral cords. On the right side, bring the topmost cord downward and using it as a **KC**, make **DHH**s around the next 3 lateral cords (see Fig. 10 for Steps 13 & 14).

14. Align the right-hand **KC** with the 7 center bundle cords. Bring the left-hand **KC** to the right under the 8 cords and make a **VDHH** around the cords.

15. On the left side, bring the topmost cord downward and using it as a **KC**, make a **DHH** around the next lateral cord. On the right side, bring the topmost cord downward and using it as a **KC**, make **DHH**s around the next 2 lateral cords (see Fig. 11 for Steps 15 & 16).

16. Align the right-hand **KC** with the 9 center bundle cords. Bring the left-hand **KC** to the right under the 10 cords and make a **VDHH** around the cords.

17. On the right side, bring the topmost cord downward and using it as a **KC**, make a **DHH** around the next lateral cord (see Fig. 12a)

18. Align the right-hand **KC** with the 11 center bundle cords. Bring the left-hand vertical cord to the right under the 12 cords and make a **VDHH** around the cords (see Fig. 13).

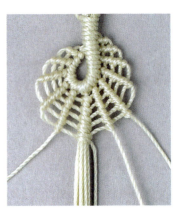
Figure 11

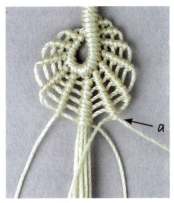
Figure 12

Figure 13

20   Margaretenspitze Designs for Jewelry

Tropical Leaf Bracelet

Figure 14

Figure 15

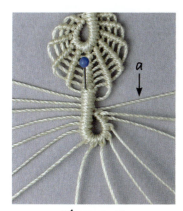

Figure 16

19. Bring the last right-hand lateral cord to the left under the bundle and make a **L.VDHH** around all the bundle cords (see Fig. 14).

Rightward Leaf

20. Take a new cord from the back center of the bundle and make a **L.VDHH** (the cord should exit to the left). Repeat until there are 13 lateral cords to the left of the bundle and one vertical **AC** remaining (see Fig. 15).

21. Thread an embroidery needle onto the **AC**. Flip the piece over and locate the 3rd lateral cord from the top. Sew through (from left to right) the bars at the base of this 3rd cord and pull the **AC** through so that the narrow bundle end is next to the upper bundle, forming a loop.

22. Flip the piece to the front again and bring the **AC** out to the right, it will now function as a **KC** (see Fig. 16a). Pin the piece so that the loop stays tightly in place. Bring the **KC** downward under the topmost lateral cord on the right and make a **DHH** around it. Continue bringing the **KC** downward and make **DHH**s around the next 4 lateral cords (see Fig. 17).

23. On the left side, take the topmost lateral cord and use it as a **KC**. Bring it down under the 2nd lateral cord and make a **DHH**. Continue bringing the **KC** downward and make **DHH**s around the next 5 lateral cords (see Fig. 17).

24. There should be one unknotted vertical cord at the bottom of the loop. Align the left-hand **KC** with this cord. Bring the right-hand **KC** to the left under both cords and make a **VDHH** around the 2 cords. This is the start of a center bundle in which all of the cords will be gathered (see Fig. 18).

25. On the right side, bring the topmost cord downward and using it as a **KC**, make **DHH**s around the next 4 lateral cords. On the left side, bring the topmost cord downward and using it as a **KC**, make **DHH**s around the next 5 lateral cords (see Fig. 19 for Steps 25 & 26).

26. Align the left-hand **KC** with the 3 center bundle cords. Bring the right-hand **KC** to the left under the 4 cords and make a **VDHH** around the cords.

27. On the right side, bring the topmost cord downward and using it as a **KC**, make **DHH**s around the next 3 lateral cords. On the left side, bring the topmost cord downward and using it as a **KC**, make **DHH**s around the next 4 lateral cords (see Fig. 20 for Steps 27 & 28).

28. Align the left-hand **KC** with the 5 center bundle cords. Bring the right-hand **KC** to the left under the 6 cords and make a **VDHH** around the cords.

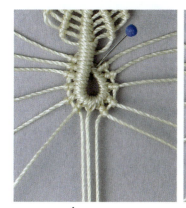

Figure 17

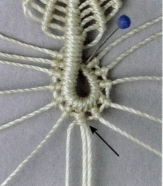

Figure 18

Figure 19

Figure 20

Joan Babcock

Project Three

Figure 21

Figure 22

Figure 23

29. On the right side, bring the topmost cord downward and using it as a **KC**, make **DHH**s around the next 2 lateral cords. On the left side, bring the topmost cord downward and using it as a **KC**, make **DHH**s around the next 3 lateral cords (see Fig. 21 for Steps 29 & 30).

30. Align the left-hand **KC** with the 7 center bundle cords. Bring the right-hand **KC** to the left under the 8 cords and make a **VDHH** around the cords.

31. On the right side, bring the topmost cord downward and using it as a **KC**, make a **DHH** around the next lateral cord. On the left side, bring the topmost cord downward and using it as a **KC**, make **DHH**s around the next 2 lateral cords (see Fig. 22 for Steps 31 & 32).

Figure 24

32. Align the left-hand **KC** with the 9 center bundle cords. Bring the right-hand vertical cord to the left under the 10 cords and make a **VDHH** around the cords

33. On the left side, bring the topmost cord downward and using it as a **KC**, make a **DHH** around the next lateral cord (see Fig. 23).

34. Align the left-hand **KC** with the 11 center bundle cords. Bring the right-hand **KC** to the left under the 12 cords and make a **VDHH** around the cords (see Fig. 24).

35. Bring the last left-hand lateral cord to the right under the bundle and make a **R.VDHH** around all the bundle cords (see Fig. 25).

Figure 25

36. Repeat Steps 3 - 19 and make another Leftward Leaf.

Part 2 - Bracelet, Left Half

37. Flip the bracelet upside down and pin in place (see Fig. 26). Untie the **OVK**. Follow the instructions for Bracelet - Part 1, Steps 3 - 36. (Fig. 27).

Figure 26

Figure 27

22   Margaretenspitze Designs for Jewelry

Tropical Leaf Bracelet

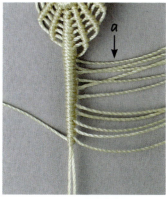
Figure 28

Figure 29

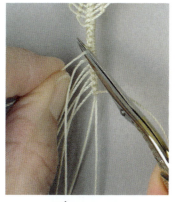

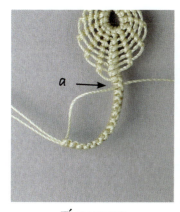
Figure 30

Part 3 - End Loops and Clasps

38. The left-hand lateral cord will be used as the **KC** for the end loop. Make a **L.VDHH** with it around all the cords.

Note - This cord should be 12" or longer, if not, pick a longer cord from the bundle to use as the **KC**. If you want a bracelet that's longer than 6 ¾", pick a **KC** that is 15" or longer and add more **HH**s in Step 41 to make a larger loop.

39. Separate a cord from the back of the bundle to be discarded and pull it outward to the right and away from the other cords (see Fig. 28a). With the **KC**, make a **R.HH**, **L.HH** around the remaining cords.

40. Repeat Step #39 until there are only 2 **AC**s remaining in the bundle (see Fig. 28). Flip the piece to the back (see Fig. 29). Carefully cut off all of the discarded cords flush with back of the bundle (see Fig. 30), leaving the **KC** and 2 **AC**s intact.

41. Lengthen the bundle with a chain of 7 **HH**s (the cord should exit to the right at the end).

42. Unpin the piece and flip it to the back. Thread the **KC** onto an embroidery needle and sew from left to right through the "spine" on the back of the bundle where it meets the lower leaf (see Fig. 31a). Continue with a few more stitches to secure the cord, sewing upward on the center back, right to left and then left to right, and so on (see Fig. 32a).

43. Thread one of the two **AC**s (choose the one closest to the front of the chain) onto a needle and sew from left to right through the spine on the back of the bundle, then sewing upward as in Step #42 (see Fig. 33a). Cut off the lower **AC** (see Fig. 33b).

44. Reduce the two remaining cords to 1 ply each. Tie them together with a tight **OVK**. Apply a tiny dab of clear nail polish. Let dry, and cut off the excess cords.

45. Repeat Steps #38 - 44 on the other end of the bracelet.

46. Attach the clasp parts to the loops with jump rings (see Figure 34).

Figure 31

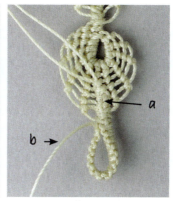
Figure 32

Figure 33

Figure 34

Joan Babcock

Oleander Earrings

Materials

Nylon Cord: Each earring requires -
   1 @ 76", 2 @ 44"
(2) Earring wires
(24) 8° Seed beads
(2) 11° Seed beads

You can substitute other beads of the same size for the bottom and center beads if you prefer. These are the ones I used:
(2) 7mm lentils (for center)
(2) 7mm teardrops
(2) 4mm spacers

Oleander Earrings

Part 1 - Top Section

1. Align the two 44" cords with the ends even. At the 22" (center) point, tie them together with a temporary **OVK** (Overhand Knot). Pin the **OVK** to the board with the cords positioned vertically (see Fig. 1a). These will be the **AC**s (Anchor Cords).

2. Pin or tape the 76" cord horizontally just under the **OVK**. There should be 33" to the left and 43" to the right of the **AC**s (see Fig. 1). This will be the **KC** (Knotting Cord). Bring it to the right under the closest **AC** and make a **VDHH**, then under the next **AC** and make a **VDHH**. The 2 **VDHH**s should be as tight and close together as possible (see Fig. 2).

3. Bring the **KC** back to the left under the rightmost **AC** and make a single **VHH** (see Fig. 3a). Bring the **KC** under the next **AC** and make a **VDHH** (see Fig. 3b).

4. Bring the **KC** back to the right make a **VDHH** around each of the **AC**s (see Fig. 4).

5. Repeat Steps #3 & 4 four more times. Bring the **KC** back to the left and make a **VDHH** around each **AC**. The **KC** should exit to the left at the top and the bottom of this chain (see Fig. 5a).

6. Remove the chain from the board and remove the **OVK**. Retighten the top **VDHH**s if they look loose. There should be 5 closed loops (they look like small bumps) on the left edge of the chain. The center loop will later be used for the earring wire (see Fig. 5b and 6a). Form the chain into a horseshoe shape and pin it to the board (see Fig. 6). The 2 **KC**s (the outermost cords) will not be used in the next step.

7. There are 4 cords in the center of the piece (see Fig. 6). Use Cords #3 & 4 (the 2 leftmost cords) as **KC**s and Cords #1 & 2 as **AC**s. Make (diagonal) **DHH**s with Cords #3 & 4 around Cord #2 (see Fig. 7), then do the same around Cord #1 (see Fig. 8, center).

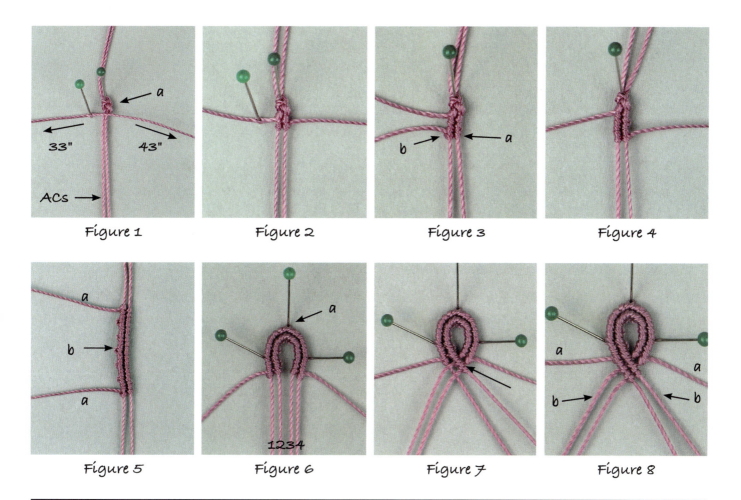

Figure 1 Figure 2 Figure 3 Figure 4

Figure 5 Figure 6 Figure 7 Figure 8

Joan Babcock

Project Four

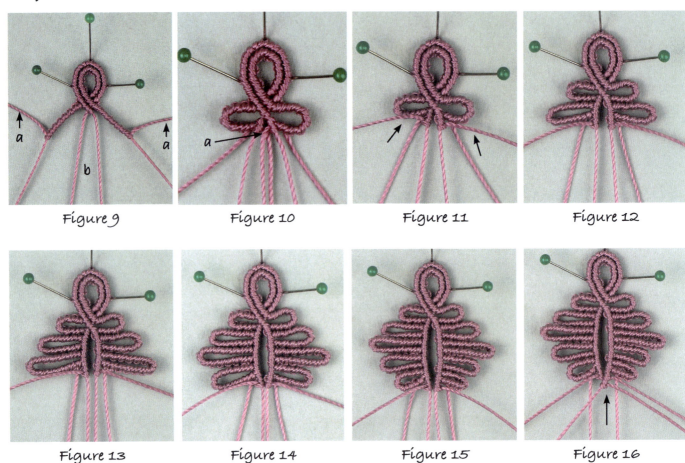

Figure 9 Figure 10 Figure 11 Figure 12

Figure 13 Figure 14 Figure 15 Figure 16

Part 2 - Side Loops

• Do the next steps on both sides of the earring.

8. Bring the **KC** (Fig. 8a) under the closest cord (Fig. 8b, this will be called the loop **AC**) and make a chain of 14 **HH**s. **Important** - the cord should exit downward on the first **HH** and upward (or outward) on the last **HH** (see Fig. 9a).

9. Bring the chain inward to meet up with the closest of the 2 center vertical cords (Fig. 9b, these will be called the main **AC**s). Using the loop **AC**, make a **VDHH** around the main **AC** (the **VDHH** cord should exit towards the center, see Fig. 10a). Bring the cord back under the main **AC** and make a **VDHH** exiting towards the outside (see Fig. 11).

10. Bring the **KC** downward under the loop **AC**. Make a **HH** chain of 22 **HH**s. The cord should exit downward on the first **HH**. Repeat Step #9 (see Fig. 12).

11. Bring the **KC** downward under the loop **AC**. Make a **HH** chain of 30 **HH**s. The cord should exit downward on the first **HH**. Repeat Step #9 (see Fig. 13).

12. Bring the **KC** downward under the loop **AC**. Make a **HH** chain of 22 **HH**s. Repeat Step #9 (see Fig. 14).

13. Bring the **KC** downward under the loop **AC**. Make a **HH** chain of 14 **HH**s. Repeat Step #9 (see Fig. 15).

Part 3 - Lower Section

14. Cross the right main **AC** over the left main **AC**. With the left cord make a (diagonal) **DHH** around the right cord (see Fig. 16).

Oleander Earrings

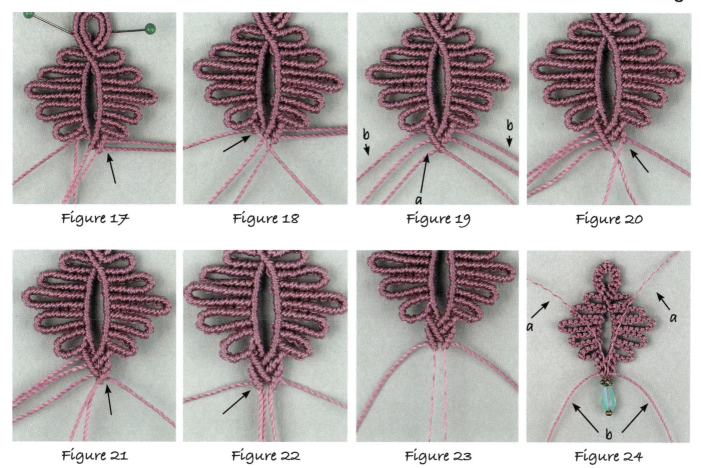

Figure 17　　　　Figure 18　　　　Figure 19　　　　Figure 20

Figure 21　　　　Figure 22　　　　Figure 23　　　　Figure 24

15. Bring this same **DHH** cord along with the cord to the right of it underneath the rightmost cord (this will be the **AC**). Make 2 side by side **DHH**s around the **AC** (see Fig. 17).

16. On the left-hand side, the leftmost cord will be the **AC**. Bring the next cord to the right under the **AC** and make a (diagonal) **DHH** around the **AC** (see Fig. 18). Make **DHH**s with the next 2 cords around the same **AC** (see Fig. 19).

17. Make an **OVK** at the end of the outermost cord (Fig. 19b) on the right and left side to mark them. On the right side, bring the outer cord downward as an **AC** and make a **DHH** around it with the next cord (see Fig. 20). Join the **DHH** cord with the **AC** and make a **DHH** around the 2 **AC**s with the next cord (see Fig. 21).

18. On the left side, bring the outer cord downward as an **AC** and make a **DHH** around it with the next cord. Join the **DHH** cord with the **AC** and make a **DHH** around the 2 **AC**s with the next cord (see Fig. 22).

19. The 2 center **DHH**s should be very tight, retighten them if necessary. Remove the earring from the board. Carefully cut off the **OVK** cord from each side flush with the end of the row. Untwist each of the remaining 2 center cords and cut off 2 plies from each cord, flush with the end of the row. This leaves 2 cords having only 1-ply (thread) each (see Fig. 23, center).

20. Put the beads of your choice on the 2 center threads with a 11° or 10° seed bead at the bottom. Flip the earring to the back. Thread a narrow sewing or beading needle onto the threads (one at a time) and sew upwards through the large beads, bypassing the seed bead at the bottom (see Fig. 24).

21. Pull the threads taut, centering the beads. The 2 threads (one on each side, Fig. 24a) will be used to sew on the remaining beads. **Optional -** run the thread(s) through beeswax to help prevent fraying.

Joan Babcock

Project Four

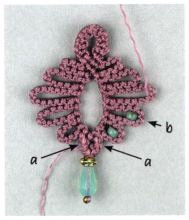
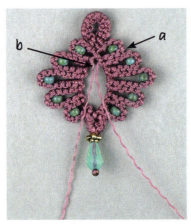
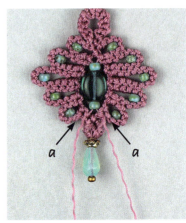

Figure 25 Figure 26 Figure 27

Part 3 - Loop and Center Beads

22. On each side: Thread a sewing or beading needle onto one of the threads. Bring the closest hanging cord (Fig. 24b) upward over the lower section of the earring. Sew around and through this cord several times to secure it. Leaving the sewing thread intact, cut off the excess from this cord so that it doesn't show at the front of the earring (see Fig. 25a).

23. Seed beads - One 8° seed bead will be sewn into the bend of each loop. To move the thread into the right location, sew along the back part of the chain making one or more stitches. Sew through the side of the chain, then through the seed bead and into the opposite side of the loop. Move on to the next loop (see Fig. 25b). **Note -** make sure that stitches are not visible when viewed from the front. Repeat until each loop has a seed bead (see Fig. 26).

24. After the last bead is sewn into the top loop, sew the thread back through the chain and downward through the seed bead so that it comes out on the lower part (chain) of the top loop (see Fig. 26a). Sew along the back of the chain towards the center. Pass the needle through the **VDHH** cords and into the center opening (see Fig. 26b).

25. Put beads on the (joined) threads. Use one bead or stack several beads to fit the opening. Sew the threads through the edges of the opening close to the bottom (see Fig. 27a).

26. Sew the threads through 2 or 3 threads at the lower center section. Tie them together with a tight **OVK** (see Fig. 28a). Apply a tiny dab of clear nail polish to the **OVK** and let dry. Cut off the excess threads.

27. Make the top/center closed loop larger by running an embroidery needle through it. Attach an earring wire through the loop (see project photo).

Figure 28

Margaretenspitze Designs for Jewelry

Oleander Bracelet

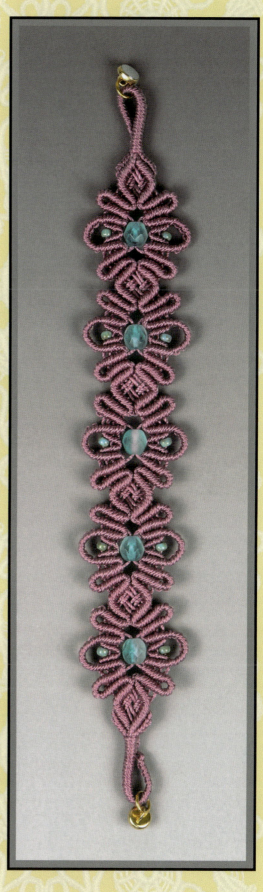

Materials

Nylon Cord: 16 @ 60"
Beads and Findings:
(6) 6mm round beads
(12) 8° seed beads
(2) 6 - 8mm jump rings
(1) Magnetic clasp

Project Five

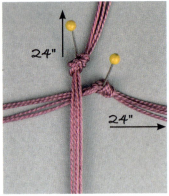

Figure 1

Figure 2

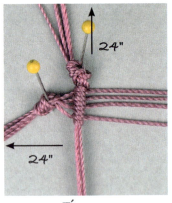

Figure 3

Part 1 - Starting the Bracelet

1. Divide the cords into four groups of 4. Make a temporary **OVK** (Overhand Knot) in each group 24" from one end to hold the cords together.

2. Left side cords - Pin one group to the board vertically with the 24" lengths facing upward. Pin another group slightly below and to the right of the first **OVK**. The cords should be horizontal and pass under the vertical bundle. **Important -** The 24" lengths must face towards the right (see Fig. 1).

3. One by one, bring each of the 4 cords from the horizontal bundle to the left and make **VDHH**s around the vertical bundle (see Fig. 2).

4. Right side cords - Pin another group to the board vertically with the 24" lengths facing upward. Pin the last group slightly below and to the left of the first **OVK**. The cords should be horizontal and pass under the vertical bundle. **Important -** The 24" lengths must face towards the left (see Fig. 3).

5. One by one, bring each of the 4 cords from the horizontal bundle to the right and make **VDHH**s around the vertical bundle (see Fig. 3).

6. Pin the knotted rows to the board in a "V" shape (see Fig. 4). The 36" cords should hang downward and the 24" cords should face upwards. Remove the 4 **OVK**s and join the upper cords in one large temporary **OVK**.

Part 2 - Flower Section

Note - The bracelet is divided into a right and a left side which are mirror images of each other. In most cases, I will give directions for the right-hand side only. After each step is completed on the right-hand side, do the same step on the left-hand side in a mirror image.

7. There are 2 bundles of 4 cords each at the center (see Fig. 4a). Take a cord from the back of the left bundle and join it with the right bundle and one from the back of the right bundle and join it with the left bundle.

8. On the right side bring the 4 bundle cords to the right and make **DHH**s around them with each of the 4 hanging cords. This row should run parallel to the row above it. Repeat on the left side (see Fig. 5).

9. Using the 4 bundle cords, make a **HH** chain of 8 **HH**s. **Note -** Choose a cord from the back as the **KC**, the other 3 cords will be **AC**s. The first **HH** should exit upward. Repeat on the left side (see Fig. 6).

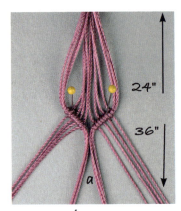

Figure 4

Figure 5

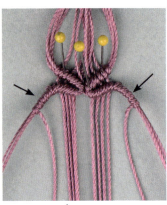

Figure 6

Margaretenspitze Designs for Jewelry

Oleander Bracelet

Figure 7

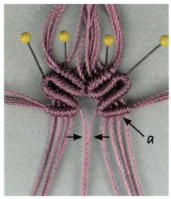
Figure 8

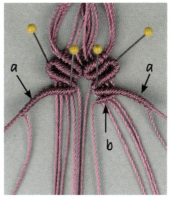
Figure 9

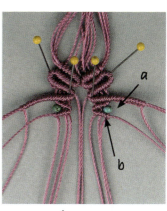
Figure 10

10. Bend the **HH** chain into a loop, the bundle cords facing towards center. Starting with the outermost hanging cord, make a row of 4 **DHH**s around the 4 bundle cords (see Fig. 7). This row should be very close to the previous row.

11. Separate one cord from each of the bundles, these 2 cords will hold the 6mm bead (see Fig. 8, center). On the right side, bring the 3 remaining bundle cords to the right and make a row of 4 **DHH**s. This row should be horizontal, but angled slightly upward (see Fig. 8a). Repeat on the left side.

12. Using the 3 bundle cords, make a **HH** chain of 12 **HH**s. Choose a cord from the back as the **KC**, the other 2 cords will be **AC**s. The first **HH** should exit upward. Repeat on the left side (see Fig. 9a).

13. On the right side, bring the outermost hanging cord towards center and make a row of 3 **DHH**s (see Fig. 9b & Fig. 10). This row should be slightly angled downward towards center. Thread an 8° seed bead onto the outermost cord (see Fig. 10a). Bring the **AC** back towards the outside and make a row of 3 **DHH**s (see Fig. 10b). This row will be at a slight angle to accommodate the bead. Repeat on the left side.

14. On each side, bring the **HH** chain back towards center and make a row of 4 **DHH**s around the bundle cords (see Fig. 11a). Thread a 6mm bead onto the 2 center cords (see Fig. 11, center).

15. On the right side, join one cord from the center bead with the 3 right-hand bundle cords. Bring these 4 cords to the right and make **DHH**s around them with each of the 4 hanging cords. This row should be angled slightly downward. Repeat on the left side (see Fig. 12).

16. On the right side, choose a cord from the back of the bundle as the **KC**, use the other 3 cords as **AC**s. Make a **HH** chain of 8 **HH**s. The first **HH** should exit upward. Repeat on the left side (see Fig. 13a).

17. Bend the **HH** chain into a loop, the bundle cords facing towards center. Starting with the outermost hanging cord, make a row of 4 **DHH**s around the 4 bundle cords. This row should be very close to the previous row (see Fig. 13b).

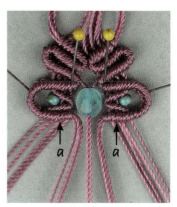
Figure 11

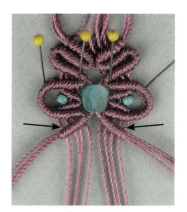
Figure 12

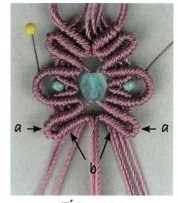
Figure 13

Joan Babcock

Project Five

Figure 14

Figure 15

Figure 16

Figure 17

Figure 18

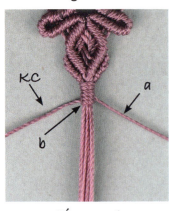

Figure 19

Part 3 - Diamond Shape Section

18. Take a cord from the back of the left bundle and join it with the right bundle and one cord from the back of the right bundle and join it with the left bundle.

19. On the right side bring the 4 bundle cords to the right and make **DHH**s around them with each of the 4 hanging cords. This row should run parallel to the row above it. Repeat on the left side (see Fig. 14).

20. Cross the 3rd & 4th hanging cords over Cds. 5 & 6 and under Cds. 7 & 8. Cross the 1st & 2nd hanging cords under Cds. 5 & 6 and over Cds. 7 & 8 (see Fig. 15).

21. Working from the outside towards center, make a row of 4 **DHH**s on each side. These rows form the bottom of the diamond shape (see Fig. 16).

Part 4 - Main Bracelet

22. Main Bracelet - Repeat Part 2 & 3 two times then flip the bracelet upside down. To start the second half of the bracelet, do Steps #20 & 21 to complete a diamond section, then repeat Part 2 & 3 two times.

Part 5 - End Loops and Clasp

23. Flip the piece to the back. Cut off one cord from each of the center bundles flush with the end of the row. This leaves 3 cords in each center bundle.

24. Flip the piece to the front and pin in place. On each side, bring the outermost cord downward as the **AC** and make a row of 3 **DHH**s, gathering all cords into the row as you go along (see Fig. 17).

25. Take a long cord from the back of one of the center bundles. You'll need a 14" cord to make the bracelet as instructed (6 ¾" length not including the jump ring and clasp). Make 2 **VLHK**s (**R.HH**, **L.HH**, **R.HH**, **L.HH**) around all other cords joining them in a single bundle (see Fig. 18).

Note - For a longer bracelet, you will need a longer **KC**. For every additional ¼" (4 **VLHK**s) you'll need an additional 3 ½" on the **KC**. In rare instances you'll have to add a new cord to use as the **KC**.

Margaretenspitze Designs for Jewelry

Oleander Bracelet

Figure 20

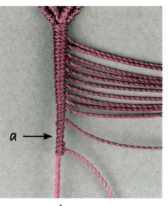
Figure 21

Figure 22

Figure 23

26. Separate a cord from the back of the bundle and pull it outward to the right and away from the other cords (see Fig. 19a). This cord (and the cords in the next step) will be cut off later. With the **KC**, make a **VLHK** (**R.HH**, **L.HH**) around the remaining cords (see Fig. 19b).

27. Repeat Step #26 until there are only 2 **AC**s remaining at the end of the bundle (see Fig. 20). Lengthen with a chain of 7 **HH**s. The cord should exit to the right at the end (see Fig. 21a). More **HH**s can be added later if needed.

28. Unpin the piece and flip it to the back. Carefully cut off all of the discarded cords flush with back of the bundle, leaving the **KC** and 2 **AC**s intact (see Figures 22 & 23).

29. Repeat Steps #25 - 28 on the other end of the bracelet. To check the length so far, form the end chains into loops as in Fig. 24. Be sure to factor in the additional length that your jump rings and clasp will add. If the end loops are too short, add as many **HH**s as needed to lengthen them.

30. On each end - Thread the **AC** that is closest to the front of the chain onto an embroidery needle. Sew from left to right through the "spine" on the back of the bundle 2 **VLHK**s down from the top of the chain (you can make it higher or lower to adjust the size of the loop). Continue working your way towards the main bracelet, sewing back and forth through the spine with a few more stitches and ending at the top of the chain (see Fig. 24a).

31. Thread the **KC** onto a needle and sew this cord in the same way as in Step #30. Cut off the remaining **AC** flush with the end of the **HH** chain. Reduce the remaining 2 cords to 1-ply each and tie them together with a tight **OVK**. Apply a tiny dab of clear nail polish and let dry. Cut off the excess.

32. Attach the clasp parts to the loops with jump rings (see Fig. 25).

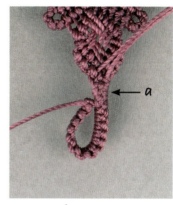
Figure 24

Figure 25

Joan Babcock

Vine Bracelet

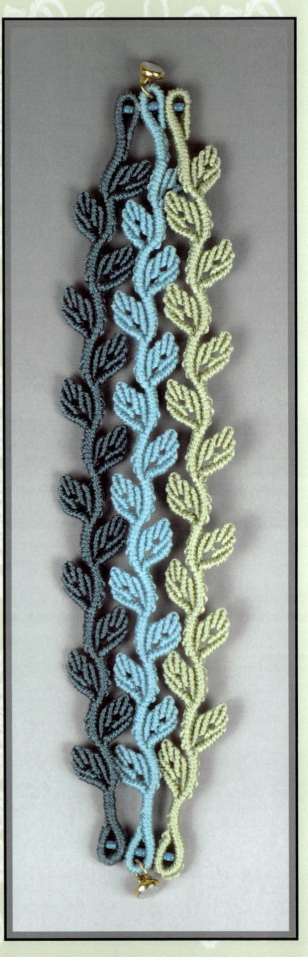

Materials

18g. Nylon Cord:
 4 @ 90" (for a single bracelet)
 12 @ 90" (for a stacked triple bracelet)
(6) 8° seed beads (for triple bracelet)
(2) 6 - 8mm Jump rings
(1) Magnetic Clasp
Sewing needle & thread

Vine Bracelet

Part 1 - Starting Loop

1. Put 2 side by side pins in your board at an upward angle (using 2 pins will keep the chain's loop large enough to thread cord through later). Drape 2 cords over the pins with the ends even. This makes four 45" cords to work with (see Fig. 1).

2. Bring the leftmost cord under the other 3 cords and make a **R.HH** (see Fig. 2a). Continue the **HH** chain with 8 more **HH**s (see Fig. 3). **Note** - to mark the 3 cords (Fig. 2b) for tightening (this is done in Step #4), mark each one at the end with a magic marker or with an **OVK** (Overhand Knot).

3. Attach a new centered cord around the 4 bundle cords with a **VDHH** (see Fig. 4). Bring the leftmost cord under the other 5 cords and make a **R.HH**. Continue the **HH** chain with 12 more **HH**s (see Fig. 5). The cord should exit to the right at the bottom.

4. Fold the chain over (see Fig. 6) and pass the **KC** through the chain loop using a needle if necessary. **Note** - To tighten the loop cords around the **KC** (if needed), pull downward on each of the 3 marked bundle cords individually. Make a **L.HH**, **R.HH** below the **HH** chain loop (see Fig. 7a).

5. Attach a new cord around the bundle cords with a **VDHH** (see Fig. 7b). Bring the leftmost cord under the other 7 cords and make a **R.HH**. Continue the **HH** chain with 4 more **HH**s. The cord should exit to the right at the bottom (see Fig. 8a).

Part 2 - Main Bracelet

6. Separate the 8 cords into two groups: 3 cords from the left side (see Fig. 9a) that will be used for the stem, and 5 cords (4 cords and the **KC**) which will be used to make the leaf (see Fig. 9b). Tape or pin the 3 stem cords out of the way for now.

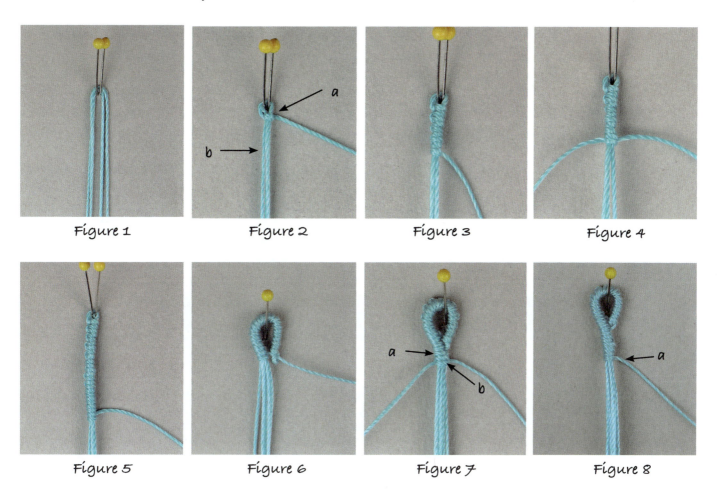

Figure 1 Figure 2 Figure 3 Figure 4

Figure 5 Figure 6 Figure 7 Figure 8

Joan Babcock

Project Six

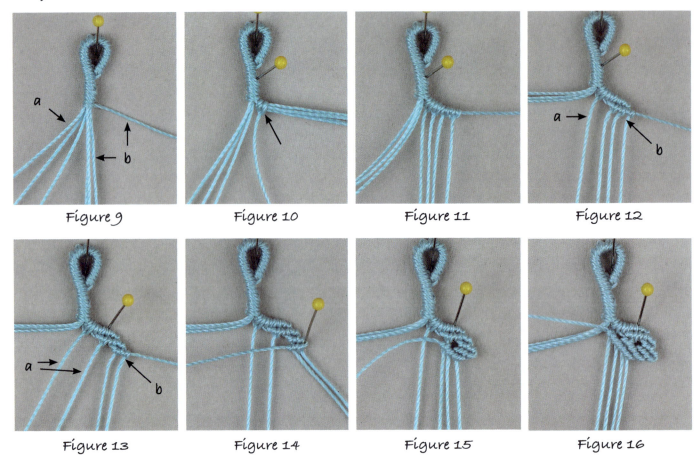

Figure 9 Figure 10 Figure 11 Figure 12

Figure 13 Figure 14 Figure 15 Figure 16

7. **Right Leaf, Row 1** - Bring the 4 cords out to the right horizontally. Bring the **KC** downward behind them and make a **DHH** (see Fig. 10). Take a cord from the back of the bundle and make a **DHH** around the 3 remaining cords. Take a cord from the back and make a **DHH** around the 2 remaining cords. Take one cord and make a **DHH** around the 1 remaining cord (see Fig. 11).

8. **Row 2** - Omit the leftmost cord from this row (see Fig. 12a). Bring the next cord to the right as the **AC** and make a row of 3 **DHH**s (see Fig. 12b).

9. **Row 3** - Omit the 2 leftmost cords from this row (see Fig. 13a). Bring the next cord to the right as the **AC** and make a row of 2 **DHH**s (see Fig. 13b).

10. **Row 4** - Put a pin in the board at the end of the row just below the **AC**. Bring the **AC** back toward center and make a row of 2 **DHH**s (see Fig. 14). Remove the pin after you make the row.

11. **Row 5** - Use the rightmost cord as the **AC** and make a row of 3 **DHH**s (see Fig. 15). **Note** - the **AC** from the previous row will be incorporated into this row as the 2nd **DHH** cord.

12. **Row 6** - Use the rightmost cord as the **AC** and make a row of 4 **DHH**s (see Fig. 16).

13. Bring the 3 stem cords downward over the **AC** of Row 6. Use the **AC** to make a **VDHH** around the stem cords (see Fig. 17a). Bring this cord downward to join the 3 stem cords. Use the leftmost leaf cord (Fig. 17b) to make a **VDHH** around the 4 stem cords. Repeat this pattern until all of the leaf cords are incorporated into the stem bundle (see Fig. 18).

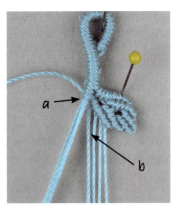

Figure 17

Figure 18

36 Margaretenspitze Designs for Jewelry

Vine Bracelet

14. **Left Leaf** - Follow Steps #7 - 13, substituting right for left and left for right in the instructions (see Figures 19 - 25). Make a total of 14 leaves for a 6 ½" bracelet (not including clasp and jump rings).

Part 3 - End Loops and Clasp

15. Continue to use the present **KC** if it is at least 14" long, if not, pick a longer cord from the bundle to use for this end loop. Add 8 **HH**s to the chain (see Fig. 26a), starting with a **L.HH** and ending with a **R.HH**.

16. Separate a cord from the back of the bundle to be discarded and pull it outward to the left and away from the other cords (see Fig. 26b). With the **KC**, make 2 **HH**s (**L.HH**, **R.HH**) around the remaining cords (see Fig. 26c).

17. Repeat Step #16 until there are only 2 **AC**s remaining in the bundle (see Fig. 26d). Leaving the **KC** and 2 **AC**s intact, carefully cut off the 5 discarded side cords flush with the bundle (see Fig. 27a).

18. Lengthen the bundle with a chain of 11 **HH**s. The last **HH** should exit to the left (see Fig. 27b).

19. Unpin the piece and flip it to the back. Thread the **KC** onto an embroidery needle. To close the loop, sew from right to left through the "spine" on the back of the bundle about a ¼" down from the top of the chain (see Fig. 28). Continue sewing upward along the spine of the chain to the top, making several passes from left to right then back again (see Fig. 29a).

20. Thread the **AC** that is closest to the front of the chain (Fig. 29b) onto the needle. Sew this cord right to left through the "spine" and upward, as with the **KC** (see Fig. 30). Carefully cut off the remaining **AC**.

21. Reduce the cords to 1-ply each and tie them together with a tight **OVK** (see Fig. 31). Apply a tiny dab of clear nail polish to the **OVK**. Let dry and cut off the excess threads.

22. If making a single rather than a triple bracelet, attach the clasp parts to the loops with jump rings.

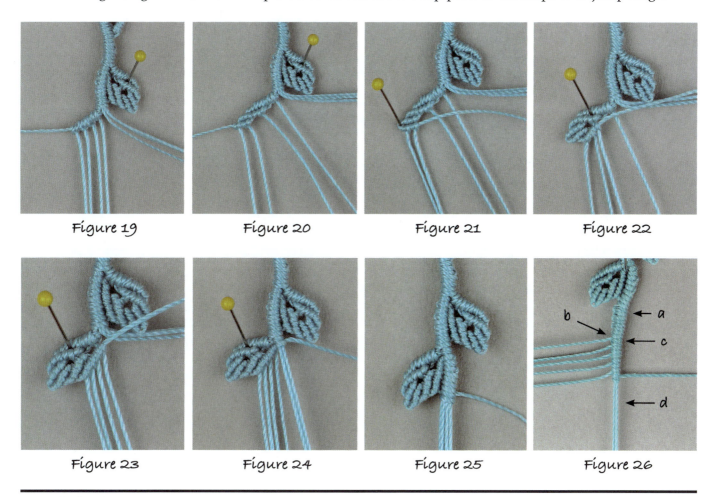

Figure 19   Figure 20   Figure 21   Figure 22

Figure 23   Figure 24   Figure 25   Figure 26

Joan Babcock

Project Six

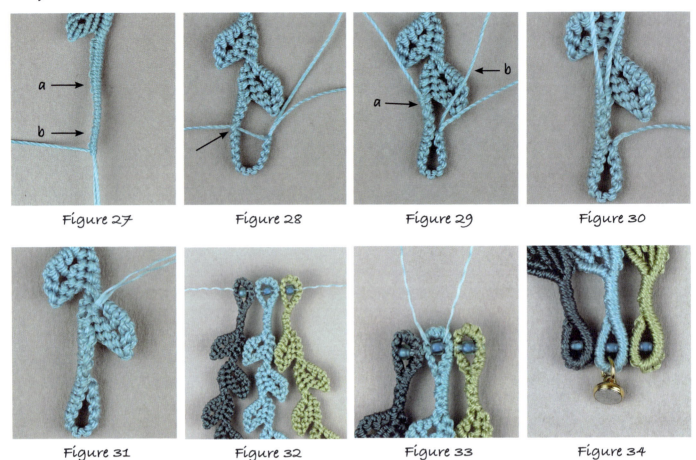

Figure 27 Figure 28 Figure 29 Figure 30

Figure 31 Figure 32 Figure 33 Figure 34

Part 4 - Stacked Triple Vine Bracelet

• Joining 3 single vine bracelets creates a wider bracelet with more visual impact. To join them together follow these steps:

23. Remove one ply from a 16" cord to use as a thread or use beading/sewing thread of your choice. Attach a sturdy sewing needle.

24. On the middle one of the 3 vines, sew through the side of the loop about mid-way between the top and the bottom. Thread an 8° seed bead onto the thread and sew through the opposite side of the loop (be sure that there is enough space above the bead to attach a jump ring later for the clasp). Adjust the thread so that there is an equal amount to the right and left of the bead (see Fig. 32, center).

Tip - Sewing through knotted chains is much easier if you use a thimble to push the needle through.

25. Line up the left vine's loop next to the middle loop and sew through the closest side of the loop. Add a bead and sew through the outside part of the loop.

26. Repeat Step #25 for the right vine with the other half of the thread (see Fig. 32).

27. On each side, sew the thread back through all loops and beads to the opposite side.

28. On each side, sew back through the outer loop and bead, then through the side of the middle loop and then the middle bead (see Fig. 33). Make an **OVK** in each thread. Apply a tiny dab of clear nail polish to the **OVK**, let dry and cut off the excess thread.

29. Attach the clasp parts to the middle loop with jumprings (see Fig. 34).

Margarete Swan

Materials

18g. Nylon Cord:
 10 @ 60"
(1) 10° seed bead
(1) 1" pin back

Project Seven

Part 1 - Swan's Head

1. Fold one cord in half and pin to the board at the center of the cord. This will provide a right and a left **AC** (Anchor Cord).

2. Center a new cord behind the **AC**s and make a **VDHH** (Vertical Double Half Hitch) around each **AC**. The **VDHH**s should be as close together as possible (see Fig. 1a).

3. On each side, bring the **KC** (Knotting Cord) inward and make a single **VHH** (Vertical Half Hitch) around the **AC** (see Fig. 2).

4. On each side, bring the **KC** outward and make a **VDHH** (see Fig. 3).

5. Repeat Step #3 (see Fig. 4).

6. Bring the 2 **KC**s downward parallel to the **AC**s. Attach a new centered cord around the 2 left vertical cords with a **VDHH**, then make a **VDHH** around the 2 right vertical cords (see Fig. 5).

Note - Use the outer left-hand cord (Fig. 5a) as the **KC** for Steps 7 - 13. The other 5 cords will be called Cds #1 - 5, according to their position from left to right.

7. Row 1 - Working towards the right, make a **VDHH** around Cd #1. Make a single **VDHH** around (joined) Cds #2 & 3 and another around (joined) Cds #4 & 5 (see Fig. 6).

8. Row 2 - Bring the **KC** back to the left. Separate Cds. #4 & 5 and make a **VDHH** around each one. Make a **VDHH** around (joined) Cds #2 & 3. Make a **VDHH** around Cd #1 (see Fig. 7).

9. Rows 3 & 4 (these two rows are identical) - Cds #1 & 2 each have a **VDHH**. Cd #3 has a (horizontal) **DHH**. Cds #4 & 5 each have a **VDHH** (see Fig. 8).

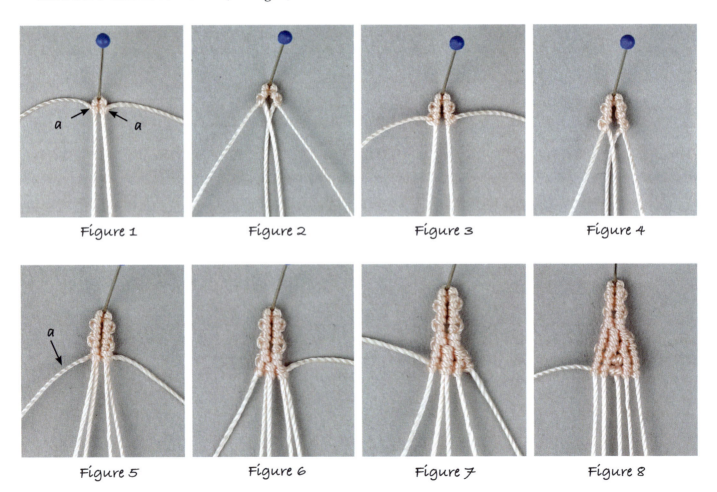

Figure 1   Figure 2   Figure 3   Figure 4

Figure 5   Figure 6   Figure 7   Figure 8

Margarete Swan

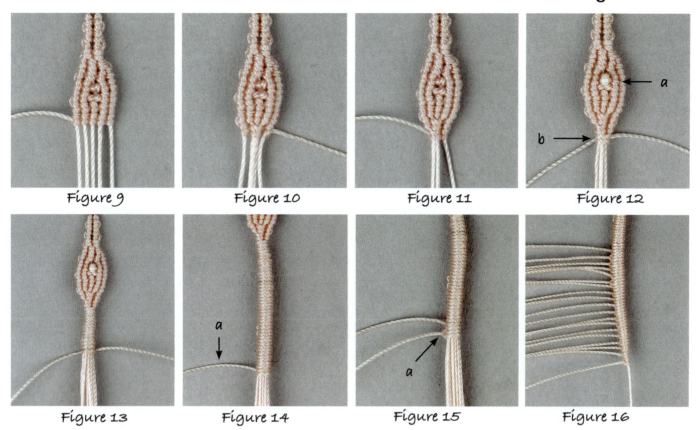

Figure 9　Figure 10　Figure 11　Figure 12

Figure 13　Figure 14　Figure 15　Figure 16

10. Rows 4 & 5 (these two rows are identical) - Make all **VDHH**s across the row (see Fig. 9).

11. Row 6 - Make a **VDHH** around Cd. #1. Make a single **VDHH** around (joined) Cds. #2, 3, & 4. Make a **VDHH** around Cd. #5 (see Fig. 10).

12. Row 7 - Make a **VDHH** around Cd. #5. Make a single **VDHH** around (joined) Cds. #1 - 4 (see Fig. 11).

13. The swan's eye can be made with either an **OVK** (Overhand Knot) or with a seed bead. Unpin the piece from the board. Thread the **KC** onto a narrow embroidery needle. Pass the needle from back to front in the valley between the 2 **DHH**s. Here you can make an **OVK** or thread on a seed bead (remove the needle to do this). Rethread and pass the needle through to the back. Straighten the seed bead and tighten the cord (see Fig. 12a).

14. Repin the piece to the board. Bring the **KC** downward to the back of the bundle.

Part 2 - Swan's Neck & Lower Body

15. Attach a new centered cord to the bundle with a **VDHH** (see Fig. 12b). Cross the 2 tails of the new cord behind the bundle.

16. Repeat the previous step until all remaining cords (6 more) are added to the bundle (see Fig. 13).

17. Take a new cord from the back of the bundle and using it as the **KC**, make a chain of 28 **HH**s around the bundle (see Fig. 14).

18. The **KC** tail should end up to the left of the bundle (if not, add a **HH**). Keep this cord separate from the bundle, it will be the first lateral cord (see Fig. 14a).

19. Take a new cord from the back of the bundle and make a **VDHH** (cord exiting to the left) around the rest of the bundle cords (see Fig. 15a).

20. Repeat the previous step to disperse all of the bundle cords, one by one, to the left of the bundle until there is only one **AC** remaining (see Fig. 16).

Joan Babcock

Project Seven

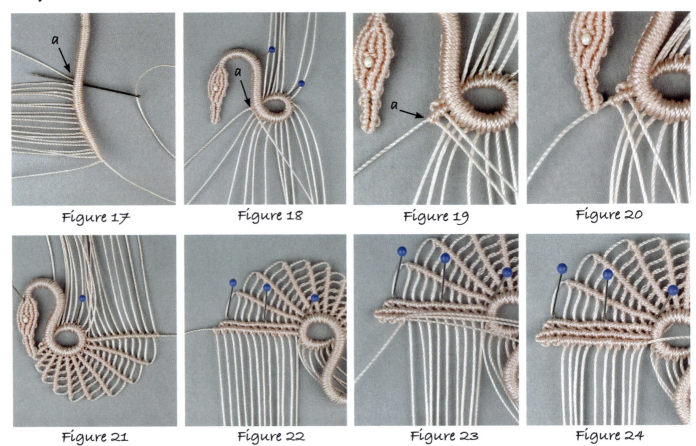

Figure 17 Figure 18 Figure 19 Figure 20

Figure 21 Figure 22 Figure 23 Figure 24

21. Unpin the piece from the board. Thread the **AC** onto an embroidery needle. Pass the needle to the left through the back side of the bundle between the first and second lateral cords (see Fig. 17a). Pull the cord completely through to the left. This cord now becomes the 2nd lateral cord.

22. Row 1 - Pin the piece to the board. Bring the first (top) lateral cord downward under the 2nd lateral cord and make a **DHH** (see Fig. 18).

23. Row 2 - Bring these 2 cords downward under the 3rd lateral cord. Make a **DHH** with the cord closest to the bundle and a **THH** (Triple Half Hitch) with the other cord (see Fig. 19a).

24. Thread the **AC** from this row onto an embroidery needle. Sew through a thread at the back of the swan's beak near the tip, pulling the beak close to the bundle (see Fig. 20). Bring the **AC** downward again to use in the next row.

25. Rows 3 - 11 - Follow the same pattern as in Step 23 to complete a total of 11 rows radiating from the bundle (see Fig. 21). In each row, the knot closest to the bundle will be a **DHH**, all other knots in the row will be **THH**s. The rows will grow progressively longer. Refer to Fig. 21 to see the correct angles of the rows. Rotate the piece as you go along to make it easier to work on.

26. Row 12 - Pin the swan to the board upside down as in Fig. 22. Bring the next lateral cord from the bundle on the left and use it as an **AC**. Make a row of **THH**s parallel to the row above it (see Fig. 22).

27. Row 13 - Bring the **AC** back towards the right (center). Make a **THH** with the 1st cord. Join this cord with the **AC** and make a **THH** with the next cord. Join this cord with the 2 **AC**s and make a **THH** with the next cord. There are now 3 **AC**s (see Fig. 23).

28. Row 13, cont. - Continue the row making **THH**s with the next 3 cords (do not gather these cords into the row). Bring one of the **AC**s to the back of the piece, leaving 2 **AC**s. Continue the row making **THH**s with the next 3 cords. Bring one of the **AC**s to the back of the piece, leaving 1 **AC**. Finish the row with **THH**s (see Fig. 24). Cut off the 2 discarded cords at the back of the piece.

Margaretenspitze Designs for Jewelry

Margarete Swan

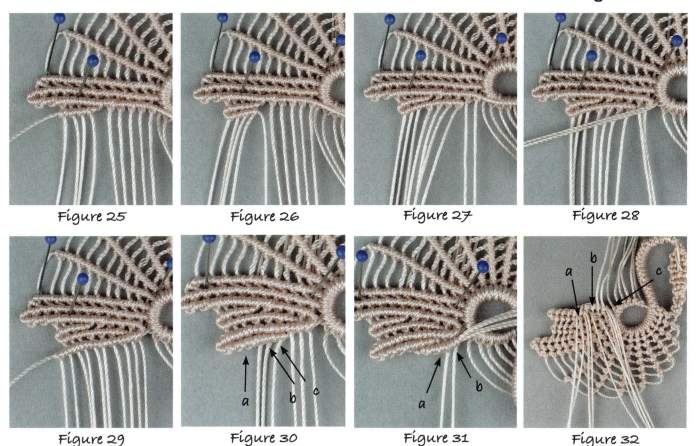

Figure 25 Figure 26 Figure 27 Figure 28
Figure 29 Figure 30 Figure 31 Figure 32

29. Row 14 & 15 - Bring the 5th cord from the left back towards the left and use it as an **AC**. Make **DHH**s with the next 4 cords (see Fig. 25). Bring the same **AC** back to the right and make **DHH**s with the next 3 cords and a **THH** with the 4th cord (see Fig. 26). Continue using this **AC** and working to the right make **THH**s with the next 3 cords. Bring the **AC** behind the piece, it will be eliminated later (see Fig. 27).

30. Row 16 - Bring the **AC** from Row 13 towards the left. Join the next lateral cord from the bundle with this **AC** (see Fig. 28). Working right to left make a row of 9 **DHH**s around the joined **AC**s. At the end of the row, make a **DHH** with one of the **AC**s around the other **AC** (see Fig. 29).

31. Row 17 - Bring the remaining **AC** back towards the right. Make a **DHH** with the 1st cord. Join this cord with the **AC** and make a **DHH** with the next cord. Repeat this pattern with the next 3 **DHH**s (see Fig. 30a). There should now be 5 **AC**s in the bundle and 6 hanging cords remaining in the row.

32. Row 17, cont. - Bring 2 **AC**s behind the piece, they will be eliminated later. Make a **DHH** with the next cord around the 3 remaining **AC**s (see Fig. 30b).

33. Row 17, cont. - Bring 2 **AC**s behind the piece. There should now be just one **AC** remaining. Make a **DHH** around it with the next cord (see Fig. 30c). Bring the **AC** behind the piece to be eliminated later.

34. Row 18 - Bring the leftmost cord to the right as the **AC** and make **DHH**s with the next 4 cords, gathering all cords into the row as you go along (see Fig. 31a). There should now be 4 **AC**s in the bundle. Make a **DHH** with the remaining hanging cord (see Fig. 31b). Bring the 4 **AC**s to the back of the piece to be eliminated later.

35. Flip the piece to the back. Cut off the 2 leftmost pairs of cords from Row 18 (see Fig. 32a) leaving about $\frac{1}{8}$" of cord. Make tight **OVK**s in each of the next 2 single cords (Fig. 32b) and cut them off leaving about $\frac{1}{4}$" of cord. Finally, reduce each of the remaining 4 cords from Row 18 (Fig. 32c) to 1 ply each. Tie the four 1-ply threads into a tight **OVK**. Cut off the excess threads, leaving about an $\frac{1}{8}$".

Joan Babcock

Project Seven

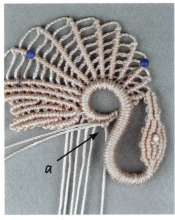

Figure 33

- Position the swan upside down. There are 8 hanging cords. To mark them for elimination, do the following: Skip the 2 leftmost cords. With a magic marker, make 4 marks at the bottom of the 3rd cord from the left. Make 3 marks on the next cord, 2 marks on the next cord, and 1 mark on the next cord. Make no marks on the rightmost 2 cords.

36. Row 19 - Bring the 2 rightmost cords to the left and make a **DHH** around them with the next cord (see Fig. 33a).

37. Flip the piece to the back. Thread the **DHH** cord onto an embroidery needle and sew through the back of the swan's neck bundle, about $3/8$" from the top of the loop (see Fig. 34). Pull the neck down closer to the body.

Figure 34

38. Row 19, cont. - Repin the piece to the board. Bring the same cord parallel to the 2 **AC**s and make a **DHH** around all 3 cords with the next cord to the left (see Fig. 35 for Steps 38 - 42). Bring one of the unmarked cords in the bundle to the back of the piece to be eliminated later. This leaves 2 **AC**s.

39. Row 19, cont. - Bring the 2 **AC**s and the **DHH** cord to the left and make a **DHH** around them with the next cord to the left. Bring one of the unmarked cords to the back of the piece to be eliminated later. This leaves 2 **AC**s.

40. Row 19, cont. - Bring the 2 **AC**s and the **DHH** cord to the left and make a **DHH** around them with the next cord to the left. Bring the cord with one mark to the back of the piece to be eliminated later. This leaves 2 **AC**s.

41. Row 19, cont. - Bring the 2 **AC**s and the **DHH** cord to the left and make a **DHH** around them with the next cord to the left. Bring the cord with 2 marks and the cord with 3 marks to the back of the piece. This leaves 1 **AC**.

Figure 35

42. Row 19, cont. - Bring the **AC** and the **DHH** cord to the left and make a **DHH** around them with the next cord to the left. This leaves 2 **AC**s and 1 **KC**. Flip the piece to the back and cut off the 5 discarded cords.

43. Row 19, cont. - Position the swan as in Fig. 36. Make a chain of 5 **HH**s with the **DHH** cord around the **AC**s (the first **HH** should exit to the left). Reposition the swan as in Fig. 37. Place a pin at the end of the **HH** chain, below the **AC**s. Bring the **AC**s back to the left and make a chain of 5 **HH**s (the first **HH** should exit to the right, or downward).

44. Flip the piece to the back. Sew one of the **AC**s and **KC** of the **HH** chain through a thread bar at the back of Row 18. Cut off the other **AC**. The **HH** chain should be in a narrow triangular shape (check it from the front). Of these 2 cords, make an **OVK** in the shortest one and cut it off. Use the remaining cord to sew on the pin backing (see Fig. 38).

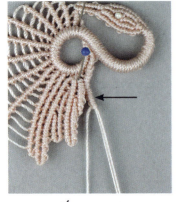

Figure 36

Fig. 37

Fig. 38

44   Margaretenspitze Designs for Jewelry

Tulip Earrings

Materials

18g. Nylon Cord:
   Each earring requires 10 @ 40"
(2) Earring Wires

Project Eight

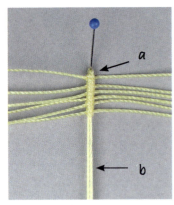

Figure 1

Tulip Center Section

1. Make an **OVK** (Overhand Knot) at the center of a cord. Pin the **OVK** to the board (see Fig. 1a) and bring the 2 cord halves downward. These two **AC**s (Anchor Cords) will be joined together and treated as a single unit (see Fig. 1b).

2. Just below the **OVK**, attach a centered cord around the **AC**s with a **VDHH** (Vertical Double Half Hitch). Repeat 5 more times, for a total of 6 attached cords (see Fig. 1). These will be called lateral cords.

3. On the right-hand side, bring the top 2 lateral cords downward parallel to the center **AC**s. Treat them as a single **AC** unit and make **VDHH**s (Vertical Double Half Hitches) with the remaining 4 lateral cords. Repeat on the left-hand side (see Fig. 2).

4. On the right-hand side, bring the top lateral cord downward and make **VDHH**s with the remaining 3 lateral cords. Repeat on the left-hand side (see Fig. 3).

5. Attach a new cord to the center 2 **AC**s with a **VDHH**. On the right-hand side, make a single **VDHH** around the 3 vertical **AC**s joining them together. Repeat on the left-hand side (see Fig. 4a).

6. Repeat Step #5 (see Fig. 4b).

7. On the right-hand side, bring the top lateral cord downward and make **VDHH**s with the remaining 4 lateral cords. Repeat on the left-hand side (see Fig. 5).

8. Position the piece horizontally with the **AC**s to the left. The lowest row has one **AC** and the row above it has 3 **AC**s. Take 2 **AC**s from the 3-**AC** row and bring them downward behind the single **AC** of the bottom row (see Fig. 6).

9. Use these 2 cords as a single **AC** unit, and bringing them to the right, make a row of 4 **DHH**s (Double Half Hitches). See Fig. 7.

10. At the end of the row, take one of the **AC**s and make a **DHH** around the other. This will make a total of 5 **DHH**s in the row (see Fig. 8).

11. Place a pin in the board at the end of the row, just below the **AC**. Bring the **AC** back to the left and make a row of 5 **DHH**s (see Fig. 9).

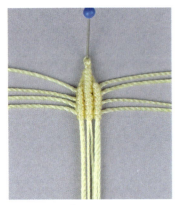

Figure 2

Figure 3

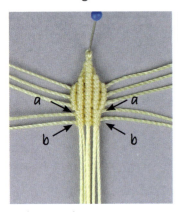

Figure 4

Figure 5

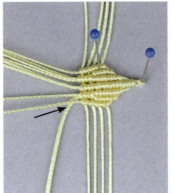

Figure 6

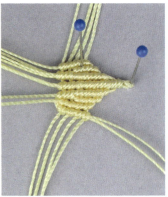

Figure 7

46   Margaretenspitze Designs for Jewelry

Tulip Earrings

Figure 8

Figure 9

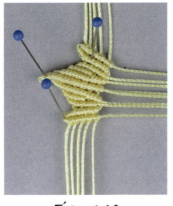
Figure 10

Figure 11

12. To complete the same steps on the opposite side of the tulip, repeat Steps 8 - 11, substituting right for left in the instructions (see Fig. 10).

13. Reposition the piece with the **AC**s hanging downward. Attach a new cord to the center 2 **AC**s with a **VDHH**. On the right-hand side, make a **VDHH** around the next single cord. Make a **VDHH** around the next 2 (joined) cords. Repeat on the left-hand side (see Fig. 11).

14. Several cords will be eliminated in the next few steps. To mark these cords, make a single **OVK** at the end of each of the top 4 lateral cords (do this on each side of the tulip).

15. On the right-hand side, bring the top 2 lateral cords downward and treat them as a single **AC** unit. Make a **VDHH** around them with the next lateral cord. Join this cord with the **AC**s and make a **VDHH** around them with the next cord. Continuing this pattern, make 2 more **VDHH**s, gathering all cords into the row. Repeat on the left-hand side (see Fig. 12a).

16. Carefully cut off 2 of the **OVK** cords from the right and left outermost bundles. **Note -** choose cords that are closest to the back of the bundle.

17. Use the leftmost lateral cord as the **KC** and bring it to the right. Make a **VDHH** around the first group of 3 cords, the next 3 (joined) cords, the 2 centermost cords, the next 3 (joined) cords, and the last group of 4 cords (this group includes the right lateral cord, see Fig. 12b).

18. Cut off one **OVK** cord from the left outer bundle. Cut off two **OVK**s cords from the right outer bundle. This leaves 2 **AC**s in each of these outer bundles. The bundle next to the outer bundle (on each side) has 3 **AC**s. Make an **OVK** at the end of one of these 3 **AC**s (see Fig. 12c).

19. Next row - Bring the **KC** to the left and make a single **VDHH** around the first 2 groups of cords, bringing them together into a group of 5 cords. Make a **VDHH** around the center 2 cords. Make a single **VDHH** around the next 2 groups of cords, bringing them together into a group of 5 cords (see Fig. 13). Cut off one of the **OVK** cords from each 5-cord bundle. This leaves 4 **AC**s in each of these outer bundles.

20. Next row - Bring the **KC** to the right and make a single **VDHH** around the first group of cords along with one of the center cords. Make a single **VDHH** around the other center cord and the remaining cords. This makes 2 side by side bundles of 5 cords each (see Fig. 14).

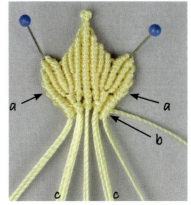
Figure 12

Figure 13

Figure 14

Joan Babcock

Project Eight

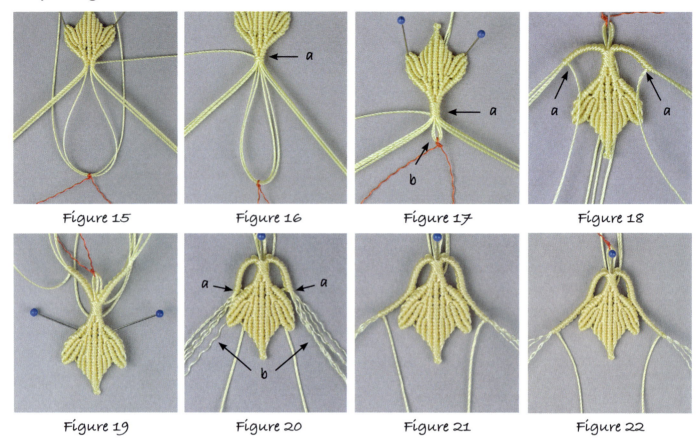

Figure 15 Figure 16 Figure 17 Figure 18

Figure 19 Figure 20 Figure 21 Figure 22

21. Take one cord from the right-hand side of the left bundle and one cord from the left-hand side of the right bundle. Bring all of the other cords off to the sides for now. Cross these 2 cords at the center, about 1 - 2" below the tulip and tie them together temporarily with a piece of spare cord. Bring the ends of the 2 cords upwards behind the other bundle cords and the tulip (see Fig. 15).

22. Bring the **KC** to the left under all cords and make a single **VDHH** around the 2 upturned cords and all other cords, grouping them together into a single bundle (see Fig. 16a). Bring the **KC** to the right and make a **VDHH**, then to the left again and make a **VDHH** (see Fig. 17a). Pull upwards on the upturned cords until they form a small loop (see Fig. 17b). **Note -** The **KC** and the 2 upturned cords will not be used in the next few steps. Keep them out of the way for now.

Side Chains

23. Position the piece as in Fig. 18. On each side, take a long cord from the bundle and make a **HH** chain of 14 **HH**s. The cord should exit in an outward (or upward) direction on the first **HH**, and an inward direction on the 14th **HH** (see Fig. 18a).

24. Flip the piece to the back. Thread the **KC** onto an embroidery needle and sew it under a thread bar on the side edge/back of the tulip. **Note -** Figure 19 shows where the needle should enter, when seen from the front of the earring. Pull the **HH** chain close to the tulip (see Fig. 20a).

25. Carefully cut off one of the 3 **AC**s from the chain (choose the cord that is closest to the back of the chain). With the 2 remaining **AC**s, untwist and separate each cord into 3 threads (see Fig. 20b).

26. Flip the piece to the front. Using the same **KC**, continue the chain with 12 more **HH**s. The cord should exit in an outward direction on the first **HH**, and an inward direction on the 12th **HH** (see Fig. 21). Cut off one of the threads at the back of the chain, leaving 5 threads intact.

27. Continue the chain with 6 more **HH**s. Cut off one of the threads at the back of the chain, leaving 4 threads intact (see Fig. 22).

Margaretenspitze Designs for Jewelry

Tulip Earrings

28. Discontinue using the **KC**. Take one of the 4 threads and using it as a new **KC**, make a chain of 21 **HH**s (see Fig. 23). The thread should exit towards the center (inward) on the first **HH**.

29. Curl the chain upward and inward in a tight circle towards the tulip so that the larger **KC** lines up with the spot where the **HH** chain is attached to the tulip (Fig. 20a). Thread this **KC** onto an embroidery needle and sew it under the thread bar on the side/back of the tulip where the **HH** chain is attached to the tulip (see Fig. 24a). Sew it under one or two other thread bars to keep it from slipping.

30. Curl the remainder of the chain in a tight circle so that it fits within the larger chain circle (the length of this chain can be adjusted with more **HH**s if necessary for a good fit). Thread the 3 **AC** threads (not the **KC**) onto a needle and sew them under the same thread bar as the larger **KC** (see Fig. 25).

31. Thread the remaining **KC** onto a sewing needle and sew through the adjacent larger chain once or twice to join the inner and outer chain parts together. Sew under the same thread bar with the other **KC** and threads (see Fig. 25). Tighten the cords and adjust the curled chain if necessary. Sew around the loose cords several times with the thread **KC** to secure them. Make an **OVK** in the thread **KC** next to the knotwork and cut off the excess along with the other loose cord and threads (see Fig. 26).

Center Loop

32. Adjust the size of the center loop (see Fig. 27a) by inserting a large embroidery needle (or other object of similar size) into the loop and tightening the cords around it. Take the leftover **KC** from the top of the center chain and sew it downward under a couple of **VDHH** cords at the bottom of the chain so that the cord lines up next to the 2 loop cords at the bottom of the chain (see Fig. 27b).

33. Untwist each of the 3 cords (see Fig. 28) and cut off 2 plies from each cord, leaving just 1 thread each. Tie these 3 threads together with a tight **OVK** (see Fig. 29). Apply a tiny dab of clear nail polish to the **OVK** and let dry. Cut off the excess threads.

34. Remove the spare cord from the loop and attach an earring wire (see Fig. 30).

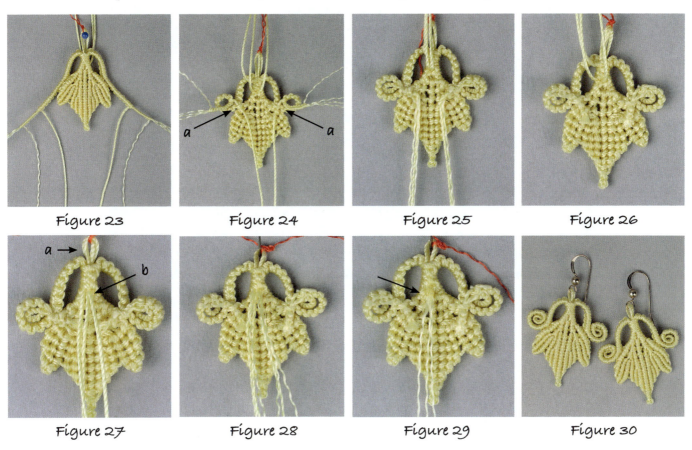

Figure 23   Figure 24   Figure 25   Figure 26

Figure 27   Figure 28   Figure 29   Figure 30

Joan Babcock

Zinnia Necklace

Materials

18g. Nylon Cord: 12 @ 85"
Beads and Findings:
(21) 6mm round , (1) 10mm round
(2) 6 - 8mm soldered rings or jump rings
(1) Clasp

Zinnia Necklace

Part 1- Flower

1. Take 3 cords and make an **OVK** (Overhand Knot) at each end (6 **OVK**s). Use these cords for the **KC**s (Knotting Cords) in Steps #2 - 4. The **KC**s will get used up much faster than the **AC**s (Anchors Cords) when making **HH** (Half Hitch) **chains**. Use only the **OVK** cords as **KC**s for any **HH** chains in Part 1.

2. Outer Petal Chain - Use one cord as the **AC** and position it vertically. Take another (**OVK**) cord to use as the **KC**, fold it in half and make a **VLHK** (Vertical Larks Head Knot) around the center point of the **AC** (see Fig. 1). Pin the **VLHK** to the board. Using the lower cord from the **VLHK** as a **KC**, make 24 **HH**s going downward. Flip the piece upside down. Use the lower **VLHK** cord as a **KC** and make 24 **HH**s in the opposite direction. The finished chain should have 50 **HH**s (see Fig. 2a).

3. Middle Petal Chain - Repeat Step #2, but make 16 **HH**s in each direction. The finished chain should have 34 **HH**s (see Fig. 2b).

4. Lower Petal Chain - Repeat Step #2, but make 14 **HH**s in each direction. The finished chain should have 30 **HH**s (see Fig. 2c).

5. Place the outer chain on top of the middle chain, so that the lowest **HH**s are even (see Fig. 3). Take the **KC** of the middle chain and make 6 **HH**s around all of the other cords (see Fig. 3a).

6. Place the joined outer and middle chains on top of the lower chain (see Fig. 4a) with the lowest **HH**s even. Take the **KC** of the lower chain and make 2 **HH**s (1 **VLHK**) around all of the other cords (see Fig. 4b).

7. Reposition the chains with the joined part facing up and the outer & middle chain ends hanging down. Repeat Step #5 to join the loose ends of the these chains (see Fig. 5a).

8. Repeat Step #6 to join the outer and middle chains with the lower chain (see Fig. 6a).

9. Pin the chains to the board as in Fig. 7. Center each of 6 new cords and attach them around the left bundle of cords with **VDHH**s (Vertical Double Half Hitches, see Fig. 7a). Attach each of the 6 cords to the right bundle, forming the two bundles into a narrow "V" shape (see Fig. 8). There should be about 1/8" (3mm) gap at the top of the "V". These 6 cords will be called the lateral cords (see Fig. 8a).

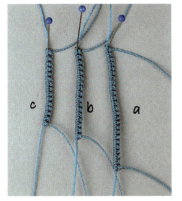

Figure 1

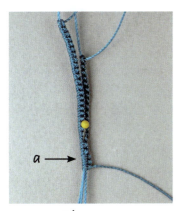

Figure 2

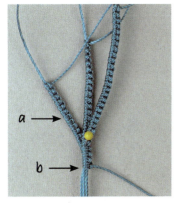

Figure 3

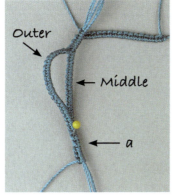

Figure 4

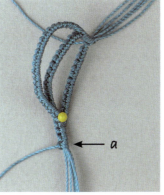

Figure 5

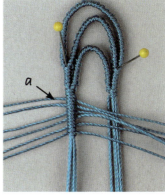

Figure 6   Figure 7

Project Nine

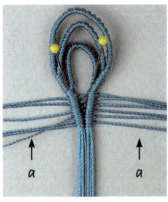

Figure 8

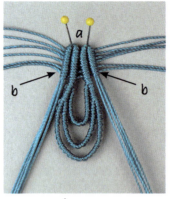

Figure 9

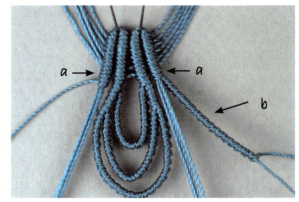

Figure 10

10. Pin the piece upside-down as in Fig. 9. Place a pin at the top left and top right of the bundles (see Fig. 9a). On each side, bring the bundle cords downward around the pin and make **VDHH**s with the 6 lateral cords, pulling the bundles close to the adjacent bundle (see Fig. 9b).

11. On each side - take one of the **OVK** cords from the 6-cord bundle and make 2 **HH**s around the other 5 cords (see Fig. 10a). Take a new cord (without an **OVK**) from the outer edge of the 5-cord bundle as an **AC** and using the same **KC** from the **HH**s, make a chain of 30 **HH**s (see Fig. 10b). This will be the lower (shortest) chain in the petal. **Note** - with this and all other **HH** chains, make sure that the "spine" is at the back, not at the side.

12. On each side - take one of the **OVK** cords from the 4-cord bundle and make 12 **HH**s around the other 3 cords (see Fig. 11a). Take a new cord (without an **OVK**) from the bundle to use as an **AC**, and using the same **KC** as was used for the 12 **HH**s, make a chain of 34 **HH**s (see Fig. 11b). This will be the middle chain in the petal.

13. On each side - make a chain of 50 **HH**s using the **OVK** cord as the **KC**. This will be the outer chain in the petal (see Fig. 12a).

14. Pin the piece as in Fig. 13. On the left side - form the outer and middle chains into curves and pin them side by side with the ends even. Using the **KC** from the middle chain, make 12 **HH**s around the other 3 cords (see Fig. 13a).

15. Position the outer and middle chains next to the lower chain and pin them side by side with the ends even. Using the **KC** from the lower chain, make 2 **HH**s around the other 5 cords (see Fig. 14). Repeat Steps #14 - 15 on the right side chains.

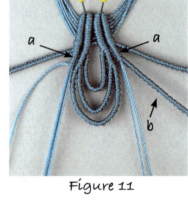

Figure 11

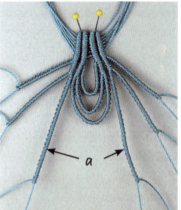

Figure 12

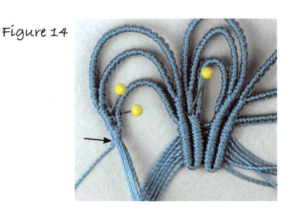

Figure 14

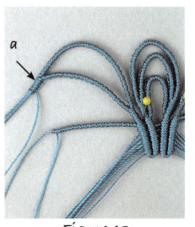

Figure 13

Margaretenspitze Designs for Jewelry

Zinnia Necklace

Figure 15

Figure 16

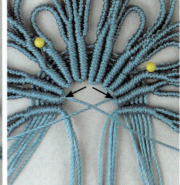
Figure 17

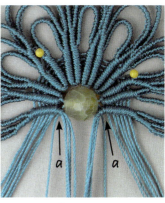
Figure 18

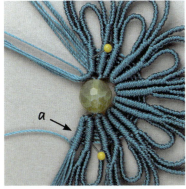
Figure 19

16. On each side - attach each of the 6 lateral cords to the outer bundle with **VDHH**s, forming the two bundles into a narrow "V" shape (see Fig. 15). There should be about $\frac{1}{8}$" (3mm) gap at the top of the "V".

17. Repeat Steps #10 - 16 twice to make two more petal sections on each side (see Fig. 16). **Note** - Use the longest **OVK** cord as the **KC** for the outer chain.

18. Center Bead - take a long cord from the back of each bundle and sew it from back to front through the inner bend of the next 2 bundles up (see Fig. 17, the cords exit here). Thread a 10mm bead onto the 2 cords so that each cord passes to the opposite side, crossing inside the bead. Pull the cords outward and then under the opposite side bundle cords. Make a **DHH** around each bundle (see Fig. 18a).

Part 2 - Neckchain

19. Using the **DHH** cord as the **KC** for all of the **HH**s in this step, start the neckchain with 2 **HH**s around the bundle (**important** - the first **HH** should exit toward the flower). Position the piece as in Fig. 19. Bring the bundle cords parallel to the previous bundle. Gather the closest lateral cord into the bundle and make 2 **HH**s around the bundle. Gather the next lateral cord into the bundle and make 2 **HH**s. Continue until all of the 6 lateral cords have been gathered into the bundle (see Fig. 19a). Pull on each of the bundle cords to bring this row closer to the adjacent row. Repeat on the left side of the flower.

Figure 20

20. Continue the chain with 2 **HH**s. Cut off one of the **OVK** cords from the bundle. Make 2 **HH**s. Cut off another **OVK** cord. Make 2 **HH**s. Cut off another **OVK** cord.

21. Flip the piece to the back and sew the **KC** through a thread bar at the base of the outer petal chain to secure the neckchain to the flower (see Fig. 20a). Flip the piece to the front again and make 2 **HH**s.

- Follow Steps 22 - 37 to make the right and the left side of the neckchain.

22. There should be 8 **AC**s (and one **KC**) remaining in the neckchain bundle. Divide the **AC**s into 2 groups of 4 cords. Using the neckchain **KC**, make 4 **HH**s around one of the groups of 4 cords. Cut off the shortest cord from this group leaving only 3 **AC**s. Take a cord from the other group of 4 and make 4 **HH**s around the other 3 cords (see Fig. 21a).

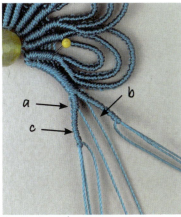
Figure 21

Joan Babcock
53

Project Nine

23. Separate out one cord from the inside of each chain (see Fig. 21b). Continue the two **HH** chains with 12 more **HH**s around the 2 **AC**s (see Fig. 21c).

24. Thread the bead onto the 2 center cords (see Fig. 22). Rejoin each bead cord with its chain and make 4 more **HH**s around the 3 **AC**s (see Fig. 22a). Pull down on the bead cords to adjust the tension if necessary. Take a new cord from the back of either chain and make 4 **HH**s around all other cords, forming a single bundle (see Fig. 23a).

25. To start the next bead segment, divide the **AC**s into a group of 3 and a group of 4. Use the previous **KC** as the **KC** for the 3-cord group. Use the longest of the 4-cord group as the **KC** for that group. Make 4 **HH**s in each chain (see Fig. 24a). **Note -** as much as possible, choose the longest cords to use as **KC**s and the shorter cords to use as **AC**s. This will keep the cords from getting used up too soon and having to add new cords.

26. Separate out one of the 3 **AC**s from the inside of each chain. Continue each **HH** chain with 12 more **HH**s (see Fig. 24b). Thread the bead onto the 2 center cords. Rejoin each bead cord with its chain and make 4 more **HH**s around each chain (see Fig. 24c). Take a new cord from the back of either chain and make 4 **HH**s around all other cords, forming a single bundle.

27. Repeat Steps 25 & 26 until there are 9 bead segments. **Note -** These instructions will make a 10 bead neckchain that is approximately 10" long on each side, not including the clasp. For a longer chain add more segments, for a shorter chain make fewer bead segments. If any cord gets too short, introduce a new replacement cord into the bundle between bead segments (Fig. 23a). Cut off the short cord after adding the new replacement cord.

28. For the final (10th) bead segment do this: Repeat Step #25. Separate out one of the 3 **AC**s from the inside of each chain. Continue each **HH** chain with 12 more **HH**s.

29. Carefully cut off one **AC** from each chain (the shortest of the 2), leaving one **AC** remaining (see Fig. 25a). Make an **OVK** at the end of each of the remaining 2 **AC**s to mark them for later elimination.

30. Rejoin each bead cord with its chain and make 4 tight **HH**s around each chain (as in Fig. 24c).

31. Choose the longer of the 2 **KC**s to use as the **KC** for the remainder of the neckchain. This cord must be at least 14" long. If it's not long enough, take another cord from the bundle to use as the **KC**.

Note - If all of the cords are too short, attach a longer replacement cord around all of the cords with a **VDHH** and use it as the **KC**. Bring the short tail of the new cord downward to join the bundle cords.

32. Make 2 **HH**s around all other cords, joining them into a single bundle. Cut off one of the **OVK** cords from the bundle. Make 2 more **HH**s. Cut off one of the **OVK** cords from the bundle. Make 2 more **HH**s. The bundle should now have only 3 **AC**s.

Note - If a new cord was added and there are more than 3 **AC**s, cut off the excess cord(s) then make 2 more **HH**s.

Figure 22

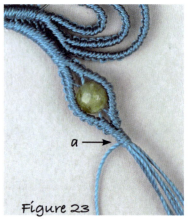
Figure 23

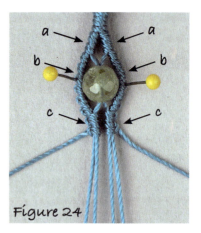
Figure 24

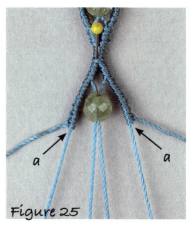
Figure 25

Zinnia Necklace

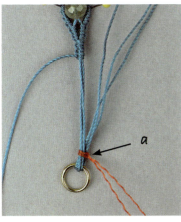

Figure 26

Figure 27

33. Pass the 3 **AC**s through a soldered ring and bring the ends upward. The ring should be 1" to 1 ½" from the lowest **HH**. Hold the cords in place by tying a spare cord around them (see Fig. 26a).

34. Gather 1 of the upturned cords into the bundle and make 4 **HH**s around all of the bundle cords (see Fig. 27a). Gather the next of the upturned cords into the bundle and make 4 **HH**s around all of the bundle cords (see Fig. 27b). Gather the last upturned cord into the bundle and make 4 **HH**s around all of the bundle cords (see Fig. 27c). Remove the spare cord.

35. For the remainder of the chain, make the **HH**s slightly looser than usual (this will make it easier to sew the threads through the chain in Step #36). Make another 6 **HH**s (you can add more to make a longer neckchain, if needed). Pull up on each of the upturned cords and start tightening, leaving a small space near the ring. Pass the **KC** through the space between the cords before completely tightening them around the ring (see Fig. 28a).

36. Tighten the 3 cords around the ring and pull the **KC** taut. Untwist the plies of the **KC** and separate them into 3 threads (see Fig. 29a). With a narrow sewing needle, sew each thread individually back under ⅜" or more of the **HH** chain (see Fig. 30a).

37. Cut off all of the excess cords flush with the neck chain (see Fig. 30b). Attach the clasp parts to the rings.

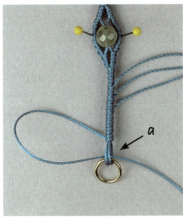

Figure 28

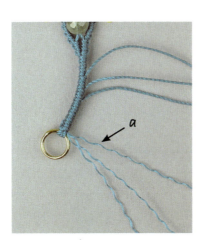

Figure 29

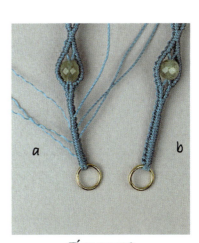

Figure 30

Joan Babcock

Swallowtail Butterfly Pin

Materials

18g. Nylon Cord: 20 @ 40"
1" Pin back finding

Swallowtail Butterfly Pin

Part I

Antennae

1. Place a thick pin (or 2 very close, side by side pins) in the board at a comfortable level for knotting. Fold a cord over so that one side is about 5" longer than the other. Drape the cord over the pin(s) with the longer part on the right. Using the right-hand cord as the **KC** (Knotting Cord), make a chain of 12 **HH**s (Half Hitches, see Fig. 1a).

2. With another cord, make a mirror image of the **HH** chain in Step #1 (see Fig. 1b). For this chain, the left-hand cord will be longer and will be the **KC**.

3. Do the following with each chain: Unpin and pass the **AC** (Anchor Cord) through the top loop and pull through to create a rounded shape (see Fig. 2a). Continue the **HH** chain below the loop intersection with 10 more **HH**s (see Fig. 2b).

Head

4. The 2 antennae should be mirror images of each other. Pin them to the board closely together. Group the 4 cords into a bundle and attach 2 centered cords around them with a **VDHH** (Vertical Double Half Hitch) (see Fig. 3a).

5. On right side, bring the upper lateral cord downward (this will be the **AC**) over the lower cord (the **KC**) and make a **HH** with the cord exiting to the outside (see Fig. 4a). Then make a **HH** in the opposite direction with the cord exiting towards the center (see Fig. 5a). Repeat on the left side (see Fig. 6a). Bring both cords under the center bundle to the opposite side.

6. With each cord, make a **HH** around the center bundle (see Fig. 6b).

7. Repeat Steps #5 & #6. On each side, make one **VHH** around the side **AC**s with the cords exiting to the outside (see Fig. 7).

8. Take a cord from the back of the center bundle and use it to make a **VLHK** (Vertical Larks Head Knot, this is a **L.HH, R.HH**) around all other cords. Tie 3 **OVK**s at the end of this cord and bring it downward to rejoin the bundle. **Note -** The **OVK**s are a way to mark a cord so that it will not be cut off when you eliminate some other cords in the upcoming steps.

9. Take another cord from the back of the 7-cord bundle and tie 3 **OVK**s at the end. Shorten the remaining 6 bundle cords to approximately 7". These shortened cords will gradually be eliminated in the upcoming steps.

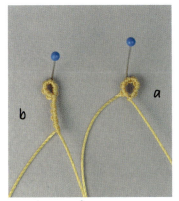

Figure 1

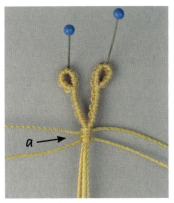

Figure 2

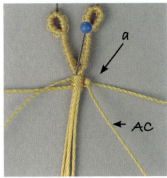

Figure 3

Figure 4

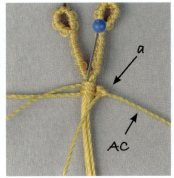
Figure 5

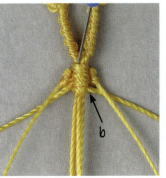
Figure 6

Figure 7

Joan Babcock

Project Ten

Figure 8

Figure 9

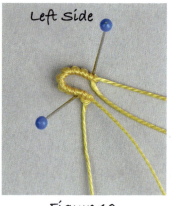
Figure 10

Figure 11

Part 2 Wings & Body

10. Take 2 cords, and at the center, make a chain of 9 **VLHK**s (18 **HH**s). The unknotted cord portions should be close to equal in length. Form the chain into a loop and pin it to the board (see Fig. 8).

11. The lower 2 cords of the chain will serve as a single **AC** unit and the upper 2 cords will be attached to the lower ones with **DHH**s. Attach the upper **AC** first, and the **KC** next to it (see Fig. 9).

12. Tie 3 **OVK**s at the end of one of the **AC**s. Shorten the other **AC** to approximately 7".

13. Repeat Steps 10 - 12 to make a mirror image of the right side (see Figures 10 & 11).

14. On each side, attach 7 cords to the joined **AC**s using **MTK**s (Mounting Knots) and push the knots closely together (see Fig. 12).

15. Pin both wing segments to the board so that they closely line up with the center segment. Using the **KC** from the center segment, make a **VLHK** around all cords to join them into one bundle (see Fig. 13a).

- **Note** - the right side wing and the left side wing will be mirror images of each other. The following directions will be for the right side wing. You will use the same directions for the left side, switching right for left in the instructions. You should complete each step on the right side, then complete the same step on the left side before going to the next step.

- There are 16 hanging cords on each side. I will refer to them as Cds. #1 - 16, going from the center to the outside edge. Cords may change position and therefore number from step to step. The number of cords will be gradually reduced as we move through the steps.

16. Using Cd. #16 as an **AC**, make a row of **DHH**s working from the outside towards center (see Fig. 13b).

17. Make a chain of 4 **AHH**s (Alternating Half Hitches, see Knot Diagrams) with the two outermost cords, Cds. #15 & 16. Leave Cd. #14 blank. Make a chain of 4 **AHH**s with Cds. #12 & 13. Leave Cd. #11 blank. Make a chain of 3 **AHH**s with Cds. #9 & 10. Leave Cd. #8 blank. Make a chain of 2 **AHH**s with Cds. #6 & 7. Leave Cd. #5 blank. Make 1 **AHH** with Cds. #3 & 4 (see Fig. 14, right).

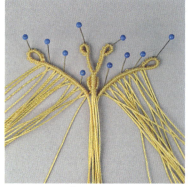
Figure 12

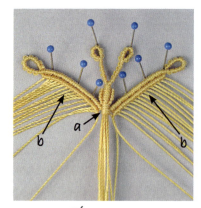
Figure 13

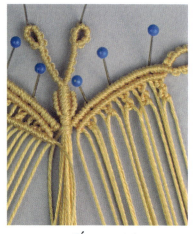
Figure 14

Swallowtail Butterfly Pin

Figure 15

Figure 16

Figure 17

18. Using Cd. #16 (the outer cord) as an **AC**, make a row of **DHH**s working towards center (see Fig. 15). Tie a single **OVK** at the end of the **AC** to mark it.

19. Bring the right side's **AC** from Step #18 to the left underneath the center bundle and make a single **HH** around the bundle. Bring this cord downward to join the bundle. Bring the left side **AC** from Step #18 to the right underneath the center bundle and make a **VLHK** around the bundle. Bring this cord downward to join the bundle.

• Count the cords in the center bundle including the **KC**. There should be 4 long cords that have 3 **OVK**s, 2 long cords that have 1 **OVK**, and 8 shorter (7") cords. Flip the piece to the back and carefully cut off 3 of the short cords flush with the **VLHK**. These 3 cords should come from the back side or the middle of the bundle, not the front where the nubs might show.

20. Repin the piece to the board. Using Cd. #15 (the outer cord) as an **AC**, make a row of **DHH**s working from the outside towards center (see Fig. 16). Tie 2 **OVK**s at the end of the **AC** to mark it.

21. Bring the right side **AC** from Step #20 to the left and make a single **VHH** around the center bundle. Bring this cord downward to join the bundle. Bring the left side **AC** from Step #20 to the right and make 2 **VLHK**s around the center bundle. This **KC** will be used again in Step 25.

22. Carefully cut off 3 more short cords from the bundle. If all of the short cords are at the front of the bundle, pull them to the back through the bundle to reposition them before cutting them off.

23. Using Cd. #14 (the outermost cord) as an **AC**, make a row of **VDHH**s working from the outside towards center (see Fig. 17, right side). The **AC** from this row will be incorporated into the next row.

24. Using Cd. #14 (the outermost cord) as an **AC**, make a row of **DHH**s working from the outside towards center (see Fig. 17, left side and Fig. 18).

25. Bring the right and left **AC**s together with the center bundle cords. Make a **VLHK** around all bundle cords using the previous **KC** (see Fig. 18).

26. Bring Cd. #5 to the right and make a **DHH** around it with Cd. #6 (see Fig. 19). Bring both Cd. #5 & #6 to the right and make a **DHH** around them with Cd. #7 (see Fig. 20). Continue this row to the right, gathering all **DHH** cords within the row as you go along (see Fig. 21a). Make the outermost knot a **THH** (Triple Half Hitch) and bring the row slightly downward (see Fig. 21b).

Figure 18

Figure 19

Figure 20

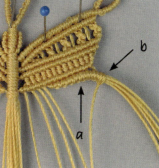

Figure 21

Joan Babcock

Project Ten

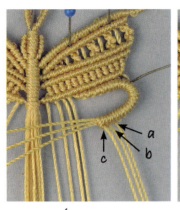
Figure 22

Figure 23

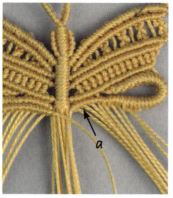
Figure 24

Figure 25

27. Make a **HH** chain of 11 **HH**s around the bundle to lengthen it, then curve it back toward center. The tail of the **KC** should exit downward (see Fig. 22a). Cut off one cord from the back of the this bundle.

28. Take a cord from the back of the bundle and make a **DHH** (see Fig. 22b). Cut off another cord from the back of the bundle.

29. Repeat Step #28 (see Fig. 22c).

30. Take a cord from the back of the bundle and make a **DHH**. Repeat. There should be only 1 **AC** remaining (see Fig. 23).

31. Bring the **AC** upward to meet Cd. #4 and make a row of 4 **DHH**s towards center. Bring the **AC** together with the center bundle (see Fig. 24a, right side).

32. Cut off the 2 remaining short cords from the center bundle.

33. Using Cd. #9 (the outermost cord) as an **AC**, make a row of **DHH**s working from the outside towards center (see Fig. 25). Bring the **AC** together with the center bundle.

34. Using the previous center bundle **KC**, make a **VLHK** around all the cords in the bundle (see Fig. 25, center). Cut off the 2 cords with 1 **OVK** at the end and 1 cord with 2 **OVK**s at the end from the center bundle.

35. Bring Cd. #8 towards center and make a **DHH** around it with Cd.#7. Make a **DHH** around both cords with Cd.#6. Repeat this pattern with the next 2 cords. Bring the bundle downward and make a **THH** with the next cord (see Fig. 26). With the same cord, make a **DHH** in the opposite direction so the cord hangs downward. **Note** - The hanging Cds. #1 & 2 are not included in this bundle.

36. Position the bundle cords facing outward. Take a cord from the back of the bundle and make a **DHH**. Repeat until there is only one **AC** remaining (see Fig. 27). Thread the **AC** onto an embroidery needle and sew through the edge of the large loop next to the **DHH** row (see Fig. 28).

Figure 26

Figure 27

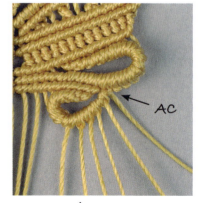
Figure 28

Margaretenspitze Designs for Jewelry

Swallowtail Butterfly Pin

Figure 29

37. Bring the **AC** downward and make a **DHH** around it with the next cord. Make **DHH**s with the next 4 cords, gathering all of the other **DHH** cords into this bundle (see Fig. 29).

38. Using the same **KC**, make a chain of 2 **HH**s. Cut off a cord from the back of the bundle.

39. Repeat Step #38 twice (see Fig. 30a). There should be 2 **AC**s remaining.

40. Bring the **AC**s upward and make tight **DHH**s with Cds. #2 & #1 (see Fig. 30b). Carefully cut off one of the **AC**s flush with the last **DHH**. Make an **OVK** at the end of the remaining **AC**. Bring the **AC** together with the center bundle.

41. Using the previous bundle **KC**, make a tight **VLHK** around all the cords in the center bundle. Cut off 4 cords from the back of the bundle (any of them except the 2 that have a single **OVK** at the end).

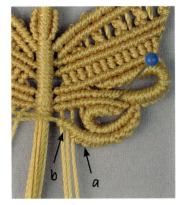

Figure 30

Part 3 Lower Wings

42. There should be 8 cords remaining in the center bundle including the **KC**. Divide them into two groups of 4 cords.

43. Bring the right-hand 4 cords parallel to the lowest row of knots on the right. Make a **DHH** around them with the 3 hanging cords, gathering all of the **DHH** cords into the bundle (see Fig. 31). Cut off one of cords (with 3 **OVK**s) from the bundle.

44. Using the same **KC** (if this **KC** is too short, use a longer cord from the bundle instead), make a chain of 12 **HH**s. The cord tail should exit to the inside, if not add a **HH** (see Fig. 32). Tighten the last **HH** and cut off the 2 shortest cords from the bundle. There should be 3 cords remaining in the bundle not including the **KC**.

45. Using only the 3 bundle cords and leaving out the inside facing **KC** (see Fig. 33a), make a chain of 10 **HH**s using the longest of the 3 as the new **KC**. The cord tail should exit to the outside on the last **HH**, if not add a **HH** (see Fig. 33b).

Figure 31

Figure 32

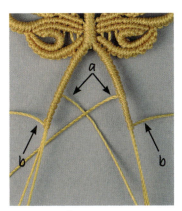

Figure 33

Joan Babcock

Project Ten

Figure 34

Figure 35

Figure 36

46. Curl the 10 **HH** chain to the outside and then back toward the main chain where the inside-facing **KC** is located. Bring the 2 **AC**s over the top of the main chain so that they are horizontal and parallel to the inside facing **KC**. Bring the new **KC** under the chain and make a **VLHK** around the 3 other cords (see Fig. 34).

47. Continue the chain upward (rotate the piece for easier knotting if necessary) with 10 more **HH**s. Cut off the shortest bundle cord. Continue the chain with 6 more **HH**s, making sure the last **HH** is very tight. Bring all the cords to the back of the piece (see Fig. 35).

48. Flip the piece to the back. On each side, thread one **AC** onto an embroidery needle and sew it through the lower back edge of the center bundle so that it forms a graceful shape for the lower wing (see Fig. 36). Sew the **KC** through the same space. Pull the cords taut and cut off the remaining **AC**.

49. Reduce both cords to 2 plies and tie them together with a tight **OVK** (see Fig. 37). Apply a tiny dab of clear nail polish to the **OVK** and let dry. If you prefer not to use nail polish, weave the thread ends into the back side of the piece and cut off the excess.

50. Sew a pin back finding to the center of the butterfly (see Fig. 38). Alternatively, attach jump rings and neck chains to the side loops to make a necklace.

Figure 37

Figure 38

Margaretenspitze Designs for Jewelry

Lunaria Bracelet

Materials

18g. Nylon Cord:
Main bracelet color - 8 @ 90" (*4 per side) and 8 @ 50" (*4 per side)
Main Flower color - 2 @ 60" (*1 per side)
Flower embellishment color - 2 @ 40" (*1 per side)
*The bracelet is composed of a right and a left side that are joined at the center.

(4) 4mm round beads
(2) 6 - 8mm jump rings
(1) Clasp, magnetic or claw style

Project Eleven

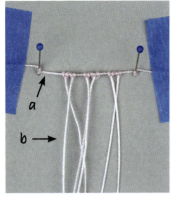

Figure 1

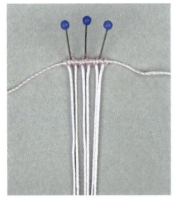

Figure 2

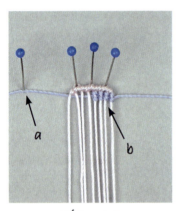

Figure 3

Part 1 - Flower

1. With a centered 90" cord, make a temporary bar between 2 pins. Tape the cord at both sides to hold it (see Fig. 1a). Fold three 90" cords in half and attach each of them to the bar cord with a **MTK** (Mounting Knot), Fig. 1b.

2. Tighten the **MTK**s and push them together. Pin them to the board through the "bump" at the top/back/center of each **MTK** (see Fig. 2). Remove the pins & tape that hold the bar cord. Bring the bar cords downward on each side to join the other 6 vertical cords.

- The vertical cords will serve as the **AC**s (Anchor Cords) and will be called Cords (Cd) #1 - 8, from left to right.

3. Row 1 - Center the 60" cord behind the **AC**s and hold it in place with a pin (see Fig. 3a). Working from the center towards the right, make **VDHH**s around Cds. #5 - 8 (see Fig. 3b). Remove the pin and working from the center towards the left, make **VDHH**s around Cds. #4 - 1 (see Fig. 4a).

4. Row 2 - Bring the left-hand **KC** (Knotting Cord) to the right and make **VDHH**s around Cds. #1 - 4 (see Fig. 5a). Bring the right-hand **KC** to the left and make **VDHH**s around Cds. #8 - 5 (see Fig. 6a). Bring the 2 **KC**s from the center to the back behind the **AC**s (see Fig. 6, side arrows).

5. Row 3, right side - Using the **KC** from the left-hand side of Row 2, continue working to the right and make a **VDHH** around Cd. #5. Make a single **VDHH** around Cds. #6 & 7, joining them together. Make a **VDHH** around Cd. #8 (see Fig. 7a).

6. Row 3, left side - Using the **KC** from the right-hand side of Row 2, continue working to the left and make a **VDHH** around Cd. #4. Make a single **VDHH** around Cds. #2 & 3, joining them together. Make a **VDHH** around Cd. #1 (see Fig. 7b).

7. Make 2 of these: Take two 50" cords and fold them in half. At the center, attach one of the cords to the other with a **MTK**. Pin each of these side sections next to the center section as in Fig. 8. This will add 4 **AC**s to each side.

- **The vertical cords will now be called Cds. #1 - 16, starting from left to right.**

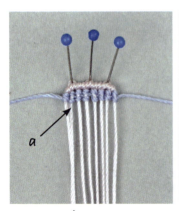

Figure 4

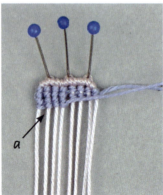

Figure 5

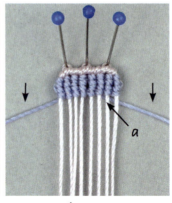

Figure 6

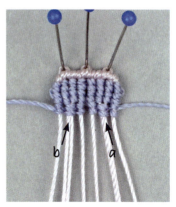

Figure 7

Margaretenspitze Designs for Jewelry

Lunaria Bracelet

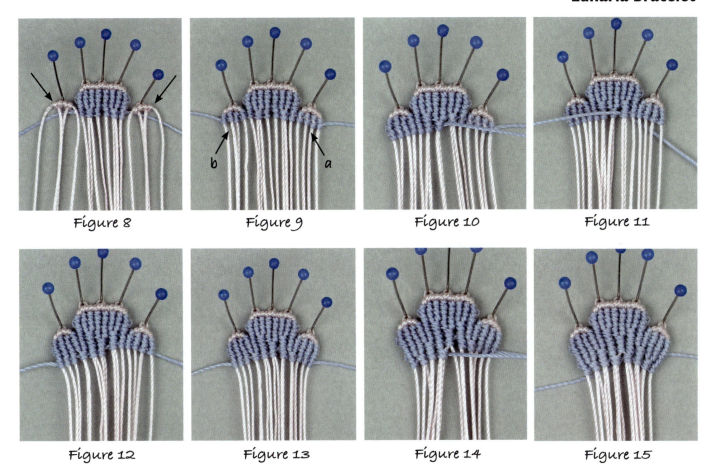

Figure 8 Figure 9 Figure 10 Figure 11

Figure 12 Figure 13 Figure 14 Figure 15

8. Row 3, continued - On the right-hand side, continue the row with **VDHH**s around Cds. #13, 14, 15, & 16 (the right side section, Fig. 9a). Make sure that there isn't a gap between the center and side sections. On the left-hand side, continue the row with **VDHH**s around Cds. #4, 3, 2, & 1 (see Fig. 9b).

9. Row 4, left side - Bring the left-hand **KC** to the right and make **VDHH**s around Cds. #1 - 5. Make a **VDHH** around joined Cds. #6 & 7, and make a single **VDHH** around Cds. #8 & 9, joining them together (see Fig. 10, left side).

10. Row 4, right side - Bring the right-hand **KC** to the left and make **VDHH**s around Cds. #16 - 12. Make a single **VDHH** around joined Cds. #11 & 10 (see Fig. 11, right side).

11. Row 5, left side - Continue using the same **KC** from Step 10 and working to the left, make a **VDHH** around joined Cds. #8 & 9. Make a **VDHH** around joined Cds. #6 & 7. Make a **VDHH** around Cds. #4 & 5, joining them together. Make **VDHH**s around Cds. #3, 2, & 1 (see Fig. 12, left side).

12. Row 5, right side - Using the other **KC** from Step 10 and working to the right, make a **VDHH** around joined Cds. #10 & 11. Make a **VDHH** around Cds. #12 & 13, joining them together. Make **VDHH**s around Cds. #14, 15, & 16 (see Fig. 13, right side).

13. Row 6, left side - Bring the left-hand **KC** to the right and make a **VDHH** around Cd. #1. Make a single **VDHH** around Cds. #2 & 3, joining them together. Make a **VDHH** around joined Cds. #4 & 5. Bring Cds. #6, 7, & 8 together and make a **VDHH** around them, joining the 3 cords together (see Fig. 14, left side).

14. Row 6, right side - Bring the right-hand **KC** to the left and make a **VDHH** around Cd. #16. Make a **VDHH** around Cds. #14 & 15, joining them together. Make a **VDHH** around joined Cds. #12 & 13. Bring Cds. #9, 10, & 11 together and make a **VDHH** around them, joining the 3 cords together (see Fig. 15, right side).

Joan Babcock

Project Eleven

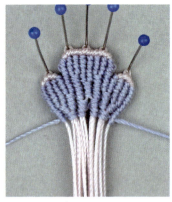

Figure 16

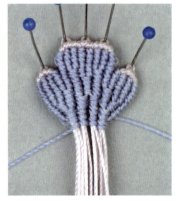

Figure 17

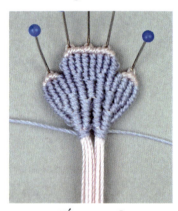

Figure 18

15. Row 7, left side - Continue using the same **KC** from Step 14. Working to the left, make a **VDHH** around joined Cds. #6, 7 & 8. Make a single **VDHH** around Cds. #2 - 5, joining the 4 cords together. Make a **VDHH** around Cd. #1 (see Fig. 16, left side).

16. Row 7, right side - Working to the right, make a **VDHH** around joined Cds. #9, 10, & 11. Make a single **VDHH** around Cds. #12 - 15, joining the 4 cords together. Make a **VDHH** around Cd. #16 (see Fig. 16, right side).

17. Row 8, left side - Bring the left-hand **KC** to the right and make a single **VDHH** around Cds. #1 - 5. Make a **VDHH** around Cds. #6 - 8 (see Fig. 17, left side).

18. Row 8, right side - Bring the right-hand **KC** to the left and make a single **VDHH** around Cds. #12 - 16. Make a **VDHH** around Cds. #9 - 11 (see Fig. 17, right side).

19. Row 9 - Make a single **VDHH** around Cds. #1 - 8. Make a single **VDHH** around Cds. #9 - 16 (see Fig. 18).

Part 2 - Curvy Chain

20. Take a long cord (see note below) from the back of the left-hand group of 8 cords to use as the **KC**. Starting with a **R.VHH**, make a chain of 43 **HH**s around all of the cords including the flower **KC**s. The last **HH** should exit to the right (see Fig. 19). Cut off the 2 flower **KC**s at the bottom of the chain.

Note - There are some long cords and some shorter cords among the bundle cords. When a new **KC** is required, always pick a long cord.

21. Form the chain into a tight curve so that the end of the chain meets the beginning. Flip the piece to the back (see Fig. 20). Thread the **KC** onto an embroidery needle and sew through a thread bar in the spine of the opposite chain (see Fig. 20a) to pull the two parts tightly together. Sew back through the spine in the opposite direction through the thread bar right next to the first one.

22. Flip the piece to the front. Make sure that the chain parts are pulled tightly together (as in Fig. 21a), and make a **VDHH** around the bundle cords. Make a **HH** chain of 30 **HH**s. The last **HH** should exit to the left (Fig. 21 shows the chain after it is formed into the next curve).

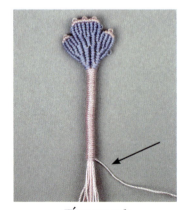

Figure 19

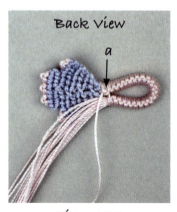

Figure 20

Figure 21

Margaretenspitze Designs for Jewelry

Lunaria Bracelet

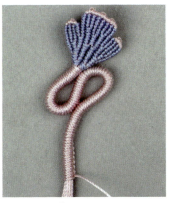
Figure 22

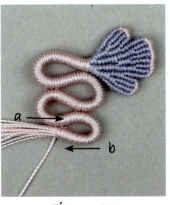
Figure 23

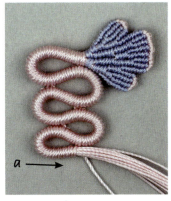
Figure 24

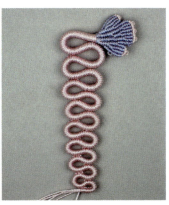
Figure 25

23. Form the chain into a tight curve to the left (see Fig. 21b). Flip the piece to the back. Thread the **KC** onto an embroidery needle and sew through the spine of the opposite chain to pull the two parts tightly together. Sew back through in the opposite direction through the next thread bar. Make an **OVK** (Overhand Knot) at the end of the **KC** to mark it for later elimination.

24. Flip the piece to the front. Choose a new long cord from the back of the bundle to be the **KC**. Starting with a **R.VHH**, make a **HH** chain of 27 **HH**s around all cords including the old **KC** (see Fig. 22). **Note -** After you have completed 10 **HH**s, pull down on the old **KC** to tighten up the place where the chains are connected.

- **Note -** as the chain progresses it should become gradually narrower. Each curve should be (slightly) less wide than the one above it (see Fig. 25). Compare your piece to the photos after you complete and attach each section of chain to be sure that it is forming the right shape.

25. Form the chain into a tight curve to the right (see Fig. 23a). Flip the piece to the back. Thread the **KC** onto an embroidery needle and sew through the spine of the opposite chain to pull the two parts tightly together. Sew back through in the opposite direction through the next thread bar.

26. Flip the piece to the front. Starting with a **L.VHH**, make a **HH** chain of 27 **HH**s around all cords. Cut off the **OVK** cord from the bundle cords.

27. Form the chain into a tight curve to the left (see Fig. 23b). Flip the piece to the back. Thread the **KC** onto an embroidery needle and sew through the spine of the opposite chain to pull the two parts tightly together. Sew back through in the opposite direction through the next thread bar. Make an **OVK** at the end of the **KC**.

28. Repeat Step #24, but make a chain of 25 **HH**s instead of 27.

29. Repeat Step #25 (see Fig. 24a).

30. Flip the piece to the front. Starting with a **L.VHH**, make a **HH** chain of 25 **HH**s around all cords. Cut off the **OVK** cord from the bundle (see Fig. 25 for Steps 20 - 51).

31. Repeat Step #27.

32. Repeat Step #24, but make a chain of 23 **HH**s.

33. Repeat Step #25.

34. Flip the piece to the front. Starting with a **L.VHH**, make a **HH** chain of 23 **HH**s around all cords. Cut off the **OVK** cord from the bundle and also one other cord from the back of the bundle. This leaves 11 bundle cords.

35. Repeat Step #27.

Project Eleven

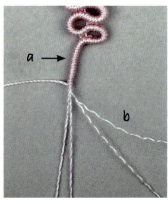

Figure 26

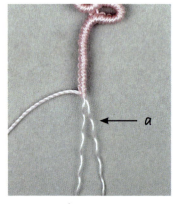

Figure 27

Figure 28

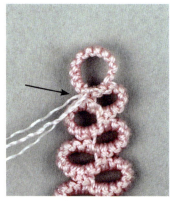

Figure 29

36. Repeat Step #24, but make a chain of 21 **HH**s.

37. Repeat Step #25.

38. Flip the piece to the front. Starting with a **L.VHH**, make a **HH** chain of 21 **HH**s around all cords. Cut off the **OVK** cord from the bundle and also one other cord from the back of the bundle. This leaves 9 bundle cords.

39. Repeat Step #27.

40. Repeat Step #24, but make a chain of 19 **HH**s.

41. Repeat Step #25.

42. Flip the piece to the front. Starting with a **L.VHH**, make a **HH** chain of 19 **HH**s around all cords. Cut off the **OVK** cord from the bundle and also one other cord from the back of the bundle. This leaves 7 bundle cords.

43. Repeat Step #27.

44. Repeat Step #24, but make a chain of 17 **HH**s.

45. Repeat Step #25.

46. Flip the piece to the front. Starting with a **L.VHH**, make a **HH** chain of 17 **HH**s around all cords. Cut off the **OVK** cord from the bundle and also one other cord from the back of the bundle. This leaves 5 bundle cords.

47. Repeat Step #27.

48. Repeat Step #24, but make a chain of 15 **HH**s.

49. Repeat Step #25.

50. Flip the piece to the front. Starting with a **L.VHH**, make a **HH** chain of 15 **HH**s around all cords.

51. Form the chain into a tight curve to the left. Flip the piece to the back. Thread the **KC** onto an embroidery needle and sew through the spine of the opposite chain to pull the two parts tightly together. Sew back through in the opposite direction through the next thread bar.

52. End Loop - Make a chain of 6 **HH**s. Cut off one cord from the back of the bundle. Make 4 more **HH**s. Cut off one cord from the back of the bundle. Make 4 more **HH**s. Cut off one cord from the back of the bundle. There should be 2 **AC**s remaining (see Fig. 26a).

53. Continue the chain with 6 more **HH**s. **Note -** for a larger loop, you can add as many **HH**s here as needed. Remove 1 ply (thread) from each of the 2 **AC**s (see Fig. 26b) Cut them off, leaving two 2-ply cords.

54. Make 2 more **HH**s. Remove 1 ply from each of the 2 **AC**s and cut them off, leaving two 1-ply threads (Fig. 27a). Add 2 more **HH**s to the chain.

55. Form the chain into a loop. Flip to the back and sew the **KC** through the spine of the adjacent chain. Sew the **AC** threads through the chain next to the **KC** (see Fig. 28). Remove 1 ply from the **KC** and cut it off.

56. Sew the **KC** and the **AC** threads through the chain spine 2 or 3 times to move them to the left side as in Fig. 29.

Lunaria Bracelet

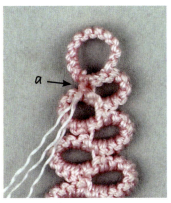
Figure 30

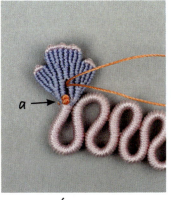
Figure 31

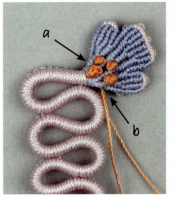
Figure 32

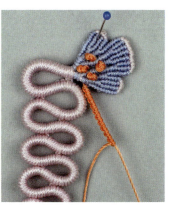
Figure 33

57. Remove 1 ply from the **KC**. Make a **OVK,** joining the 3 threads. Apply a tiny dab of clear nail polish (see Fig. 30a). Let dry and cut off the excess threads.

58. Flower Embellishment - Thread 40" of contrasting color cord onto a narrow embroidery needle. Bring the ends together and tie them with a tight **OVK**. Apply a tiny dab of clear nail polish and let dry. Cut off the excess cord $\frac{1}{8}$" from the **OVK**.

59. Sew the cord through the center/base of the flower to the front. Make an **OVK** on the front of the flower (see Fig. 31a). The **OVK** should not be overly tight. Sew through to the back. Repeat, and make an **OVK** $\frac{1}{8}$" above the first one and one **OVK** to each side (see Fig. 32a).

60. At the back, sew the cords through a thread bar at the lower side of the flower, next to the curve in the chain (see Fig. 32b).. Cut the cord into 2 equal lengths and remove the needle. Starting with a **L.VHH**, make a **HH** chain of 21 **HH**s. The last **HH** should exit to the left (see Fig. 33).

61. Curve the chain upward and back inward toward the flower. Sew the **AC** through the same thread bar where the cords exited. Sew the **KC** through a thread bar slightly above it (see Fig. 34a).

62. Bring the 2 cords to the other side and sew through a thread bar at the lower edge (Fig. 34b shows where). Make another **HH** chain of 21 **HH**s (the first **HH** should exit towards the main chain). Repeat Step #61 (see Fig. 35a).

63. Reduce both cords to 2-ply each and make an **OVK** in each cord at the back. Apply clear nail polish and let dry. Cut off the excess cords.

64. Repeat Steps #1 - 63 to make the second half of the bracelet.

65. To join the two halves of the bracelet together, position them as in Fig. 36. The top side petal of each flower should rest on top of the curve of the opposite bracelet half (see Fig. 36, arrows). Using a 1-ply piece of cord in the same color as the main chain, sew the petals to the chains on each side with several stitches.

66. **Optional -** Using a 1-ply piece of cord in the same color as the flower's side chains, sew beads into the centers of the 4 loops (see project photo).

67. Attach the clasp parts to each end with jump rings.

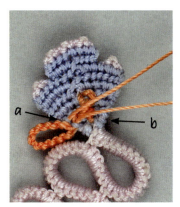
Figure 34

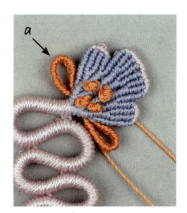
Figure 35

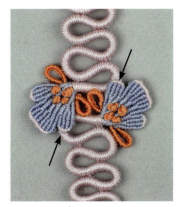
Figure 36

Joan Babcock

Phoenix Necklace

Materials

18g. Nylon Cord:
  17 @ 100", 1@ 40" for fringe beads (optional)
(1) 40mm Gemstone Donut
Variety of small beads for donut embellishment, for
  example, 8° and 10° seeds, 3 - 7mm assorted beads
(2) 6 - 8mm jump rings or soldered rings
(1) Clasp

Phoenix Necklace

Part 1 - Wing Section, Right Side

1. Attach 7 cords to the donut with **MH**s (Mounting Hitches). Pin the piece to the board with the cords hanging downward (see Fig. 1).

2. Row 1 - Bring the 2 leftmost cords to the right and treating them as a single **AC** unit, make a row of 12 **DHH**s (see Fig. 2).

3. At the end of the row, attach a new cord to the 2 **AC**s with a **MH**. Bring the right-hand cord of the **MH** to the right along with the two **AC** cords (see Fig. 3a). These 3 cords will not be used until Part 3 and should be kept separate from the "wing" pattern in the following steps.

4. Make one **VLHK** with the leftmost cord around the next cord to the right (see Fig. 4a).

5. Row 2 - The left cord of the **MH** will be used as the **AC** for this row (see Fig. 4b). Bring this cord to the left and make a row of 12 **DHH**s (see Fig. 5). **Note -** in Rows 2 - 11 of this pattern, keep each new row close to the previous row for the first 3 **DHH**s and then very gradually widen to the width of the **VLHK** at the end of the row.

6. Rows 3 - 11 - Make a **VLHK** using the **AC** of the previous row around the leftmost cord (see Fig. 6a). Use the rightmost cord as the **AC** (see Fig. 6b) and make a row of **DHH**s. Rotate the piece as necessary for ease of knotting (see Fig. 7).

7. Rows 12 - 14 - These rows do not have a **VLHK** between them and are close together (see Fig. 8).

Part 2 - Wing Section, Left Side

8. Attach 7 cords to the left side of the donut with **MH**s. Pin the piece to the board with the cords hanging downward (see Fig. 9 for Steps 8 - 10).

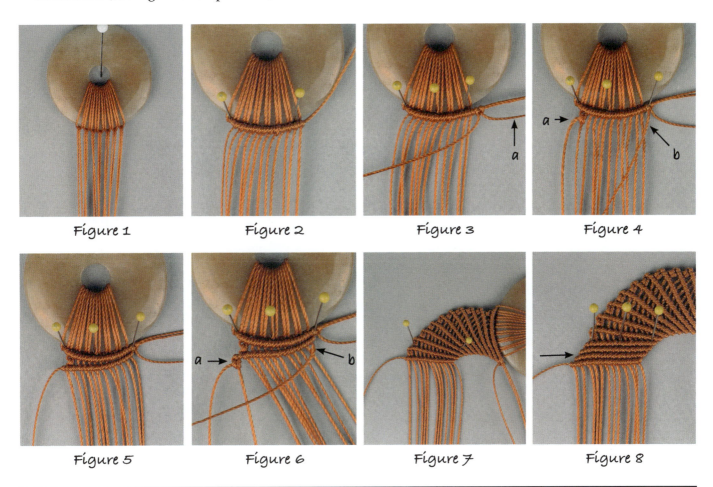

figure 1 figure 2 figure 3 figure 4
figure 5 figure 6 figure 7 figure 8

Joan Babcock

Project Twelve

9. Row 1 - Bring the rightmost 2 cords to the left and using them as a double **AC**, make a row of **DHH**s.

10. At the end of the row, attach a new cord to the 2 **AC**s with a **MH**.

11. Bring the left-hand cord of the **MH** to the left along with the two **AC** cords. These 3 cords will not be used until Part 3 and should be kept separate from the "wing" pattern in the following steps.

12. Row 2 - Make one **VLHK** with the rightmost cord around the next cord to the left (see Fig. 10a). The right cord of the **MH** will be used as the **AC** for this row. Bring this cord to the right and make a row of 12 **DHH**s (see Fig. 10).

13. Rows 3 - 11 - Make a **VLHK** using the **AC** of the previous row around the rightmost cord. Use the leftmost cord as the **AC** and make a row of **DHH**s (see Fig. 11a).

14. Rows 12 - 14 - Use the leftmost cord as the **AC** and make a row of **DHH**s (see Fig. 11b).

Part 3 - Center Section

15. Put a pin in your board and drape a cord over it (ends should be even). With the right cord, make a **HH** around the left cord. Do not tighten completely around the pin, but rather leave a loop that's large enough for 2 cords to pass through. With the left cord, make a **HH** around the right cord (see Fig. 12a).

16. Thread a few beads of your choice onto the cord. I recommend small beads such as 8° seeds, 4 - 6mm beads and small spacers (see Fig. 12b). Check to see that they fit in the area between the donut hole and the donut edge and adjust if necessary. Attach the bead cords to the center of the donut between the wing sections, passing the cord ends through the top loop (see Fig. 13, top center).

17. Position the piece with the donut on top. There should be 1 ¾" between the inside edges of Row 14 of each section (see Fig. 13, arrows).

18. With the 3 loose cords on the top right and left, make chains of 9 **HH**s. The **KC**s should exit toward the center after the last **HH** (see Fig. 14a). Thread a small bead onto the 2 center cords (see Fig. 14b).

Figure 9

Figure 10

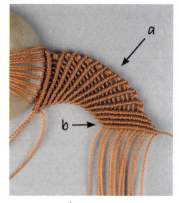

Figure 11

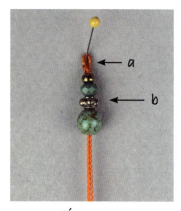

Figure 12

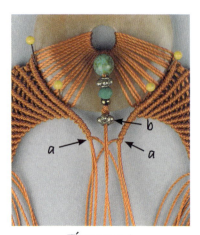

Figure 14

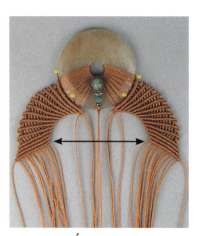

Figure 13

Margaretenspitze Designs for Jewelry

Phoenix Necklace

19. Make a **DHH** with the right-hand center cord (from the bead strand) around the 3 right-hand chain cords (see Fig. 15a). Make a **DHH** with the left-hand center cord around the 3 left-hand chain cords (see Fig. 15b).

20. Cross the left **KC** to the right under the two 3-cord bundles and make a **VDHH** around the right-hand bundle. Cross the right **KC** to the left under the two 3-cord bundles and make a **VDHH** around the left-hand bundle (see Fig. 16a).

21. Repeat Step #20 two more times (see Fig. 16b). Separate the bundles and make **HH** chains of 27 **HH**s on each side (see Fig. 17).

22. Make **DHH**s around each chain with the innermost hanging cord on each side (see Fig. 18). Check to see if the chains are the correct length (they should make the same shape as in the photo) and adjust by adding or subtracting **HH**s if necessary. On each side, continue the row of **DHH**s, gathering all cords into the row as you go along (see Fig. 19).

Part 4 - Leaf Neckchain

Note - Steps 23 - 33 are for the right side of the neckchain (Fig. 19a). The left side (19b) will be a mirror image of the right side. The left side is made in the same way, however you will need to substitute right for left and vice versa in the instructions (for example, make a **L.HH** instead of a **R.HH**, etc...).

23. Cut off 1 cord from the interior or back of the bundle, leaving 16 cords to work with.

24. Leave the **KC** out to the left (see Fig. 20a). Take a cord from the back of the bundle and make a **R.HH** around the remaining bundle cords. Leave this cord out to the right (see Fig. 20b). Take a cord from the back of the bundle and make a **L.HH**. Leave this cord out to the left. Repeat, alternating **HH**s from side to side until all bundle cords are dispersed and there is just one **AC** remaining (see Fig. 21). Bring the **AC** to the right to join the other right-hand lateral cords so that there are an equal number of lateral cords on the right and left sides.

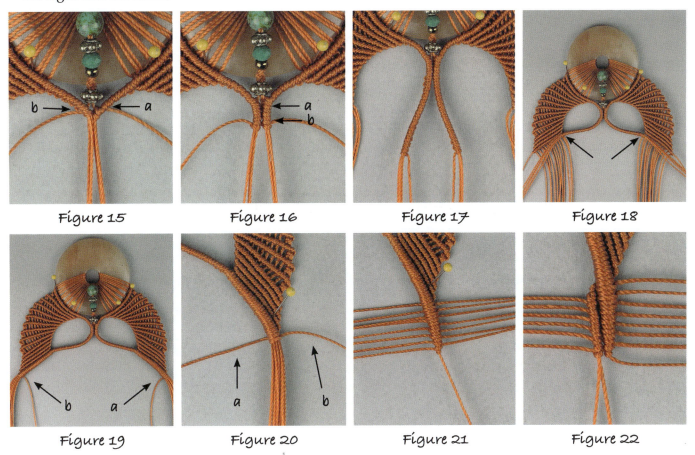

Figure 15   Figure 16   Figure 17   Figure 18

Figure 19   Figure 20   Figure 21   Figure 22

Joan Babcock

Project Twelve

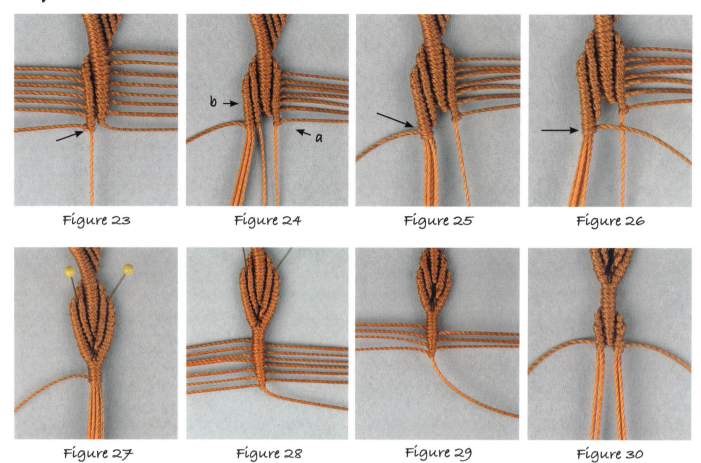

Figure 23   Figure 24   Figure 25   Figure 26

Figure 27   Figure 28   Figure 29   Figure 30

25. Bring the top left lateral cord downward parallel to the bundle. Make a **VDHH** around it with the 2nd lateral cord. Bring both of these cords downward and using them as a single **AC** unit, make **VDHH**s with the remaining left lateral cords (see Fig. 22). To extend the row, make a **VDHH** with one of the **AC**s around the other **AC** (see Fig. 23). There should be just one **AC** remaining. Repeat on the right-hand side of the leaf (see Fig. 24a).

26. Bring the top left lateral cord downward parallel to the bundle. Make a **VDHH** around it with the 2nd lateral cord. Bring both of these cords downward and make a **VDHH** around them with the 3rd cord. Continue the row of **VDHH**s, gathering all cords into the row (see Fig. 24b). Use the **AC** from the previous vertical row for the final **VDHH** (see Fig. 25). Bring the **KC** towards the center and make a **HH** around the bundle (see Fig. 26). Repeat on the right-hand side of the leaf.

27. Take a long cord from the back (either side) and join all cords together with 6 **HH**s starting with a **R.HH** (see Fig. 27). Cut off 2 cords from the back of the bundle.

28. Repeat Steps 24 - 27 to make two more leaf shapes. **Note -** The 2nd leaf will have 14 cords (7 lateral cords per side, see Fig. 28) and the 3rd leaf will have 12 cords (6 lateral cords per side).

29. Make the next 3 leaf shapes using 10 cords each (do not cut off any cords between these leaf shapes!).

30. Cut off 2 cords from the back of the bundle. Make the next 3 leaf shapes using 8 cords each (do not cut off any cords between these leaf shapes!).

31. Next leaf - repeat Step #24 so that there are 4 lateral cords on each side (see Fig. 29). Bring the top left lateral cord downward parallel to the bundle. Make a row of **VDHH**s, gathering all cords into the row (see Fig. 30). Bring the **KC** towards the center and make a **HH** around the bundle (see Fig. 31a). Repeat on the right-hand side of the leaf.

Phoenix Necklace

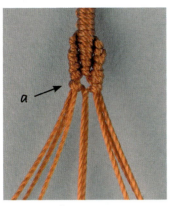

Figure 31

Figure 32

Figure 33

32. Take a long cord from the back (either side) and join all cords together with 6 **HH**s starting with a **R.HH** (see Fig. 32). **Note -** The instructions will produce a neck chain that measures approximately 8" from the necklace center on each side (this does not include jump rings and clasp). If you prefer a shorter neck chain (7" per side), skip the next step.

33. Repeat Step #31 & 32 two times. If you want a neck chain that is longer than 8", add more leaf shapes here.

Part 5 - End Loops and Clasps

34. Right Side Neck Chain - The left-hand lateral cord will be used as the **KC** for the end loop. Add 7 more **HH**s to the chain. The last **HH** should exit to the right (see Fig. 33).

35. Separate a cord from the back of the bundle (to be discarded later) and pull it outward to the left and away from the other cords (see Fig. 34a). With the **KC**, make a **L.HH**, **R.HH** around the remaining cords.

36. Repeat Step #35 until there are only 2 **AC**s remaining in the bundle (see Fig. 34). Leaving the **KC** and 2 **AC**s intact, carefully cut off the 5 discarded side cords flush with the bundle (see Fig. 35).

37. Lengthen the bundle with a chain of 7 **HH**s. The last **HH** should exit to the left (see Fig. 35).

38. Unpin the piece and flip it to the back. **Optional -** Thread a soldered ring onto the chain (or you may add a jump ring later if preferred). Thread the **KC** onto an embroidery needle. To close the loop, sew from right to left through the "spine" on the back of the bundle about a $\frac{1}{4}$" down from the top of the chain (see Fig. 36a). Continue sewing upward along the spine of the chain, making several passes from left to right then right to left (see Fig. 37).

39. Thread the **AC** that is closest to the front of the chain (see Fig. 36b) onto the needle. Sew this cord right to left through the "spine" and upward, as was done with the **KC** (see Fig. 37). Carefully cut off the remaining **AC**.

40. Reduce the cords to 1-ply each and tie them together with a tight **OVK** near the top of the **HH** chain (not shown). Apply a tiny dab of clear nail polish to the **OVK** and let dry. Cut off the excess near the **OVK**.

41. Repeat Steps #34 - 40 on the left side of the neckchain substituting right for left and vice versa in the instructions. The end loop should be a mirror image of the right side.

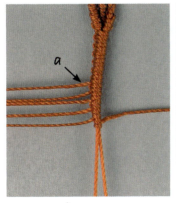

Figure 34

Figure 35

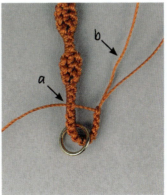

Figure 36

Figure 37

Project Twelve

42. Attach the clasp parts to the loops with jump rings.

Part 6 - Optional Fringe Beads

43. Remove one ply from a 40" length of cord. Thread a 1" strand of beads (the type of beads and the length of the strand are your choice) on to the center of the 2-ply cord. There should be a seed bead at the end of the strand. Thread half of the cord back up through the main beads, using the seed bead as a stopper (see Fig. 38a). There should be 2 equal lengths of cord coming out of the top of the bead strand.

44. Pass the cords through the center of the donut from front to back. Bring the cords downward at the back of the donut and pass them to the front through the center space above the top bead (see Fig. 38b). Tighten the cord around the donut.

45. On each side, keeping the cord loose, pass it upwards under the donut (see Fig. 39a) and bring it through the hole to the front. At the bottom edge, pass it under itself (see Fig. 39b) and tighten.

46. On each side, keeping the cord loose, bring it upward over the front of the donut (see Fig. 40a) and pass it through the hole to the back. At the bottom edge, pass it over itself (Fig. 40b) and tighten.

47. Repeat Step #45 (see Fig. 41, outer cords).

48. Thread a ¾" strand of beads onto each cord with a seed bead at the bottom. Bypassing the seed bead, thread the cord back upward through the beads and tighten (see Fig. 42).

49. Repeat Step #46. Repeat Step #45. Repeat Step #46. Repeat Step #45 (see Fig. 43, outer 4 cords on each side).

50. Thread a ½" strand of beads onto each cord with a seed bead at the bottom. Bypassing the seed bead, thread the cord back upward through the beads and tighten (see Fig. 43).

51. Flip the piece to the back. On each side, thread the cord onto a needle and sew upward under the closest thread bar at the lower edge to secure the cord. Make a tight **OVK**. Apply a tiny dab of clear nail polish and let dry. Cut off the excess cord.

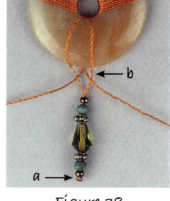

figure 38

figure 39

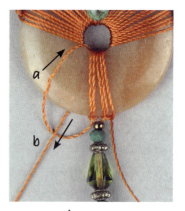

figure 40

figure 43

figure 42

figure 41

Margaretenspitze Designs for Jewelry

Sunflower
Pendant, Pin, or Bracelet

Materials

18g. Nylon Cords for the Sunflower on the Pendant, Pin, or Bracelet:
Center Coil - 1 @ 120", 2 @ 40"
Petals - 2 @ 70", 1 @ 105"

Pendant or Pin Only:
Cord for Stem - 6 @ 40", 1 @ 85"
Pendant - (1) soldered ring 8 - 10mm
Pin - 1" sew-on pin back

Bracelet Only:
Cord for Bracelet Band: 13 @ 50" and 1 @ 100"
(2) Soldered jump rings 6 - 8mm
(2) Jump rings 5 - 6mm
(1) Magnetic clasp

Twisted Rope Chain (for pendant):
Nylon Cords: 2 @ 140"
(2) 5mm soldered rings (these are small enough to fit through pendant's 8mm ring)
(1) Clasp

Project Thirteen

Part 1 - The Center Coil

1. Place a sturdy pin into your board. Fold the two 40" cords in half and drape them over the pin so that there are four 20" cords hanging from the pin. Take the 120" cord (this will be the Knotting Cord, **KC**) and measure 20" from one end. At the 20" point, make an **VDHH** around the others (the 20" part to the left) leaving a short gap between the pin and the **VDHH** (see Fig. 1).

2. Bring the 20" section of the **KC** downward with the other 20" cords. With the 100" **KC**, make a **L.VHH** around all of the 20" cords (see Fig. 2). Make a **R.VHH** and continue the chain with 6 **HH**s (see Fig. 3).

3. Remove the piece from the board. Thread the **KC** onto a needle and pass it from front to back through the loop at the start of the chain and pull through (see Fig. 4). Tighten the cords around the **KC** by pulling on them until the cords fit snugly around the **KC**.

4. Pin the piece to the board as in Fig. 5. Bring the **KC** to the left under the bundle cords and make a **L.VHH**.

5. Continue making a chain of **HH**s until the chain measures approximately 7" from top to bottom. Figure 6 shows a partially completed chain.

6. Pin down the center part well and wrap the chain around the center in a spiral. The chain should reach to point A in Fig. 7. If it's too short, add more **HH**s.

7. In the remaining portion of the chain the bundle cords will be gradually reduced. At the back of the bundle, cut off one of the cords flush with the last **HH**. Make 8 more **HH**s. Repeat this step until only one of the bundle cord remains.

8. Make **HH**s until the rope reaches to point B in Figure 7. Remove the piece from the board and flip it to the back.

9. Using a sturdy sewing needle and thread, sew the spiral together starting at the center and working outward. Sew through the spines at the back of the chains to bring the spiral together. Use a whipstitch or whichever stitch works best for you (see Fig. 8).

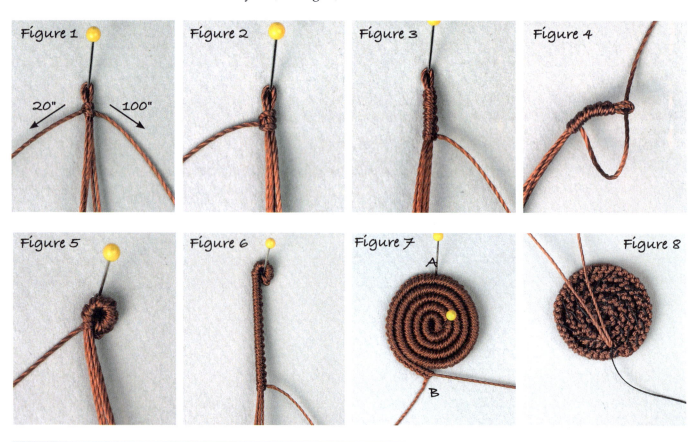

Sunflower Bracelet

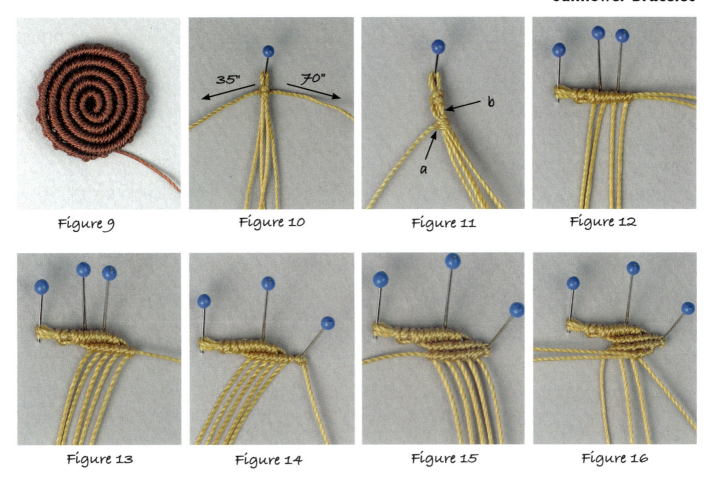

Figure 9 Figure 10 Figure 11 Figure 12

Figure 13 Figure 14 Figure 15 Figure 16

10. Sew down both cords securely at the back (see Fig. 8). Cut one of them off and leave the other one to use for sewing the coil onto the bracelet in Part 5 (see Fig. 9).

Part 2 - The Petals

11. Place a sturdy pin in your board. Fold the 70" cords in half and drape them over the pin. Make a **VDHH** around the cords with the 105" cord so that there is 35" on the left of the **VDHH** and 70" on the right (see Fig. 10). Leave a small gap (about $\frac{1}{8}$" or the same width as a **VDHH**) between the pin and the **VDHH**.

12. Bring the 35" **VDHH** cord downward to join the other four 35" cords. Bring the 70" **VDHH** cord (this will be the **KC**) to the left under the bundle and make a **L.VDHH** around the 5 cords (see Fig. 11a), leaving a small gap (about $\frac{1}{8}$" or the same width as a **VDHH**) between the 1st and 2nd **VDHH**s (see Fig. 11b).

13. Position the piece horizontally with the **KC** hanging downward. Take a new cord from the back of the bundle and make a **DHH** around the remaining 4 cords. Take a new cord from the back of the bundle and make a **DHH** around the remaining 3 cords. Take a new cord from the back of the bundle and make a **DHH** around the remaining 2 cords (see Fig. 12).

14. Take the leftmost cord and bring it to the right to use as the **AC**. Make a row of 5 **DHH**s with the 3 hanging cords and the 2 **AC**s (see Fig. 13).

15. Place a pin in the board at the end of the row, as close as possible. Make an **OVK** around the pin with the **AC** (see Fig. 14).

16. Bring the **AC** back to the left and make a row of 5 **DHH**s (see Fig. 15).

17. Bring the rightmost 2 cords to the left and make a **DHH** around them with the next cord (see Fig. 16).

Joan Babcock

Project Thirteen

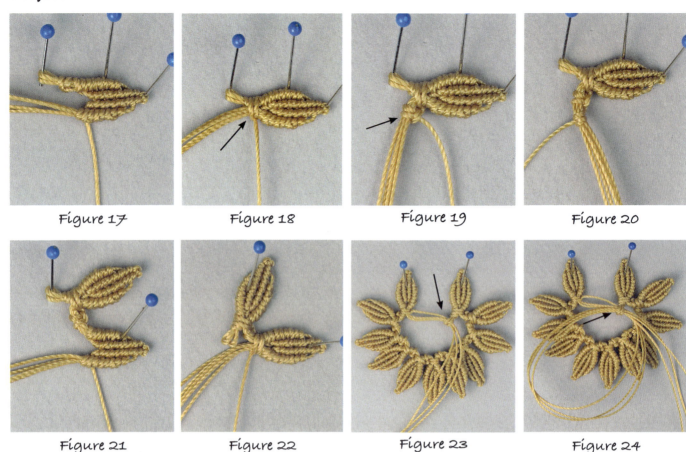

Figure 17 Figure 18 Figure 19 Figure 20

Figure 21 Figure 22 Figure 23 Figure 24

Figure 25

18. Bring the **DHH** cord to the left along with the other 2 **AC**s and make a **DHH** around the 3 cords with the next cord. Bring this **DHH** cord to the left along with the other 3 **AC**s and make a **DHH** around the 4 cords with the next cord. Bring this **DHH** cord to the left along with the other 4 **AC**s and make a **DHH** around the 5 cords with the final cord (see Fig. 17).

19. With the **KC**, make a **DHH** around all of the cords at the base of the petal (see Fig. 18). You will have to unpin the piece from the board to do this.

20. Leaving a small $\frac{1}{8}$" gap, make a **VLHK** (**L.VHH, R.VHH**) around the bundle cords (see Fig. 19).

21. Bring the **KC** to the left under the bundle and make a **L.VDHH** around the 5 cords, leaving a small gap between the **VLHK** and the **VDHH** (see Fig. 20).

22. Repeat Part 2, Steps 13 - 21 until you have 10 petals. Repeat Steps 13 - 19 to make the 11th petal. (Figures 21 & 22 show two adjoining petals).

23. Carefully trim off 3 of the bundle cords. Pass the 2 remaining bundle cords and the **KC** through the loop at the beginning of the piece (see Fig. 23). Pass all 3 cords through the loop once again (see Fig. 24).

24. Pull the cords tight around the loop and tie each one with an **OVK** (see Fig. 25). Put a dab of clear nail polish on the **OVK**s and let dry. Cut off the cords next to the **OVK**s (see Fig. 26).

Figure 26

80 Margaretenspitze Designs for Jewelry

Sunflower Bracelet

Figure 27

Figure 28

Figure 29

Part 3 - Pendant/Pin Option, Backing & Stem

25. Align the six 40" stem cords together so that all ends are even. If you want the sunflower to be a pin and do not want a ring, hold the cords together temporarily with a piece of spare cord at the center. For the pendant option, thread on an 8mm soldered ring (see Fig. 29, top). Fold the cords in half and drape them over a pin (see Fig. 27, top).

26. Position the 85" cord horizontally behind the bundle so that there is 20" to the left, and 65" to the right. Make an **VDHH** around the bundle just below the pin (see Fig. 27). Bring the 20" length downward and join it with the other bundle cords.

27. The 65" cord will be the **KC** (Knotting Cord). Make a **L.VHH**, then a **R.VHH** around the bundle (see Fig. 28).

28. Row 1 - Divide the bundle cords into 3 groups having 4, 5, & 4 cords. Working from right to left, make a **VDHH** around each group (see Fig. 29 for Rows 1 & 2). **Note -** Because there are an uneven number of cords (13) the "extra" cord will be in the group at the center of the piece.

29. Row 2 - Working from left to right, repeat the same pattern as in Row 1.

30. Rows 3 & 4 - Divide the cords into 6 groups of 2 cords (the "extra" cord should be carried along with one of the center groups, making it a group of 3 cords). See Fig. 30.

31. Rows 5 & 6 - These rows will have the following pattern: Make a single **VDHH** around the first 2 cords, joining them together. Make a **VDHH** around each of the middle 8 cords (the "extra" cord should be carried along with one these cords). Make a single **VDHH** around the last 2 cords, joining them together (see Fig. 31).

32. Rows 7 & 8 - Make 2 rows of 12 **DHH**s (see Fig. 32). Leave out the "extra" cord from of these rows, it will float at the back.

33. Rows 9 & 10 - Use the same pattern as Rows 5 & 6 (bring the "extra" cord back). See Fig. 33 for Steps 33 - 35.

34. Rows 11 & 12 - Use the same pattern as Rows 3 & 4.

35. Rows 13 & 14 - Use the same pattern as Rows 1 & 2.

Figure 30

Figure 31

Figure 32

Figure 33

Joan Babcock

Project Thirteen

Figure 34

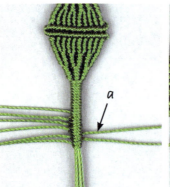
Figure 35

Figure 36

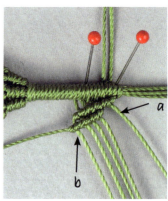
Figure 37

36. Starting with a **L.VHH**, make a chain of 13 **HH**s around the bundle (see Fig. 34a). The **KC** should exit to the left on the last **HH**. Leave this cord out to the left, it will the 1st (top) lateral cord.

37. Take a new cord from the back of the bundle and make a **L.VDHH** around all other vertical cords. Repeat twice (with new cords) so that there are 4 lateral cords on the left side of the bundle (see Fig. 34).

38. Take a new cord from the back of the bundle and make a **R.VHH**. Leave this cord out to the right (see Fig. 35a). Take a new cord from the back of the bundle and make a **L.VHH** this cord joins the other cords on the left.

39. Repeat Step 38. There should now be 6 lateral cords on the left and 2 lateral cords on the right of the stem (see Fig. 35).

40. Leaf, Row 1 - Reposition the piece as in Fig. 36. Bring the rightmost hanging cord to the left as the **AC** and make a row of 5 **DHH**s. Angle this row slightly outward from the stem (see Fig. 36a).

41. Row 2 - Skip the rightmost cord from the previous row (see Fig. 37a) and use the 2nd cord from the right as the **AC** and make a row of 4 **DHH**s (see Fig. 37b).

42. Row 3 - Skip the 2 rightmost cords and use the 3rd cord from the right as the **AC** and make a row of 3 **DHH**s (see Fig. 38a).

43. Row 4 - Skip the 3 rightmost cords and use the 4th cord from the right as the **AC** and make a row of 2 **DHH**s (see Fig. 38b).

44. Row 5 - Skip the 4 rightmost cords and use the 5th cord from the right as the **AC** and make one **DHH** (see Fig. 39).

45. Row 6 - Reposition the piece so that leaf is horizontal. Place a pin at the end of row 5, just below the **AC**. Bring the **AC** back to the right and make one **DHH** with the next cord (see Fig. 40).

46. Row 7 - Bring the leftmost cord to the right and make a row of 2 **DHH**s (see Fig. 41). **Note** - the **AC** from Row 6 will be used for the 1st **DHH**.

47. Row 8 - Bring the leftmost cord to the right and make a row of 3 **DHH**s (see Fig. 42a).

48. Row 9 - Bring the leftmost cord to the right and make a row of 4 **DHH**s (see Fig. 42b).

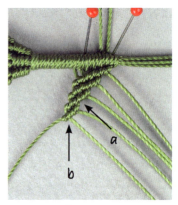
Figure 38

Figure 39

Figure 40

Margaretenspitze Designs for Jewelry

Sunflower Bracelet

Figure 41 Figure 42 Figure 43 Figure 44

Figure 45 Figure 46 Figure 47 Figure 48

49. Row 10 - In this row, the cords will gradually be gathered up into the row in the following way: Bring the leftmost cord (as the **AC**) to the right and make a **DHH** around it with the next cord. Bring the **DHH** cord to the right and join it with the **AC**. Make a **DHH** around the 2 joined cords with the next cord. Continue this pattern to complete the row, gathering all of the **DHH** cords into the row as you go along. The last **DHH** should have 5 **AC**s and 1 **KC** (see Fig. 43).

50. With the **KC**, make another **HH** in the opposite (inward) direction so that the cord exits toward the stem (see Fig. 44).

51. With the same **KC**, make a **R.DHH** around the stem bundle. This will become the 3rd lateral cord on the right (see Fig. 45a). Take a new cord from the back of the bundle and make a **R.DHH** around all vertical cords. Repeat twice. There should now be a total of 6 lateral cords on the right side of the bundle (see Fig. 45).

52. Refer to Steps #40 - 50 to make a leaf on the right side of the stem that is a mirror image of the leaf on the left side. Substitute right for left and left for right in the instructions (see Fig. 46 for Steps 40 - 44, Fig. 47 for Steps 45 - 48 and Fig. 48 for Steps 49 & 50).

53. When the leaf is complete, make a tight **L.VDHH** around all vertical cords with the **KC** (see Fig. 49). Flip the piece to the back and carefully cut off 4 of the bundle cords.

Figure 49

Joan Babcock

Project Thirteen

Figure 50

Figure 51

Figure 52

Figure 53

54. Fold 2 of the bundle cords upward (leaving about a 1" loop) and join them with the rest of the bundle. Make a **R.VDHH**, then a **L.VDHH** around all bundle cords, catching the folded cords into the bundle (see Fig. 50).

55. Repeat Step 54 three times (see Fig. 51). All of the cords should be folded up except one. Cut this leftover cord off flush with the last **VDHH**.

55. Pass the **KC** to the right through the loop (see Fig. 51a). One by one, tighten the folded cords around the **KC** leaving a small gap. Pass the **KC** once more through the loop to the right. Completely tighten the cords around the **KC** (see Fig. 52).

56. Cut off the remaining cords (Fig. 52a) flush with the stem. Untwist the **KC**, separating the 3 plies. With a narrow sewing needle, sew each of the threads (one at a time) upward through the inside of the stem (at least $\frac{1}{4}$") and then bringing the needle out to the side. Cut each thread off flush with the knotwork.

57. See Part 5 for instructions on assembling the Sunflower (Fig. 53). Instructions for the "Twisted Rope Chain", designed to hold the pendant, are at the end of this chapter.

Part 4 - Bracelet Option, Backing and Band

58. Align the thirteen 50" stem cords together so that all ends are even. Make a temporary **OVK** (Overhand Knot) at the center (25") point to join them together. Position the cords vertically and pin them to the board through the **OVK** (see Fig. 54).

59. Measure 25" from the end of the 100" cord. Bring it under the vertical cords just below the **OVK** with the 25" to the left and the 75" to the right. Make a **VDHH** around the bundled cords (see Fig. 54a).

60. Untie the **OVK** and bring the 25"cord upward and join it with the 13 cords. Retie the **OVK**. The 75" cord will be the **KC** for the backing.

61. To make the backing and the first part of the stem with leaves, follow Steps 28 - 52. When completed, the leaves will look like Fig. 55.

62. With the inward facing **KC**, make a **L.VDHH** around the stem cords. Leave this cord to the left as the 1st lateral cord for the next leaf segment (see Fig. 56a).

Figure 54

Figure 55

Figure 56

Margaretenspitze Designs for Jewelry

Sunflower Bracelet

Figure 57

Figure 58

Figure 59

Figure 60

63. Repeat Steps #37 to 52 to make another left & right leaf. With the inward facing **KC**, make a **L.VDHH** around the stem cords (see Fig. 57a).

64. Flip the bracelet around to work on the second half. Follow Steps #36 - 52 to make the first part of the stem with leaves. **Note** - Since there are already 2 **HH**s completed at the start of the stem, make only 11 **HH**s (not 13) in Step #36.

65. With the inward facing **KC**, make a **L.VDHH** around the stem cords. Leave this cord to the left as the 1st lateral cord for the next leaf segment.

66. Repeat Steps #37 to 52 to make another left & right leaf. With the inward facing **KC**, make a **L.VDHH** around the stem cords.

End Tabs and Clasp

67. Place the partially completed band around your wrist and measure the gap between each end. To determine the additional length of knotted chain to make on each end, do the following: Measure the length of your clasp + jump rings and subtract that from the gap length. For example: Gap = 3″, Clasp + jump rings = 1". Therefore 3″- 1" = 2". Next, divide that number in half to get the length you will add to each end of the bracelet (2"÷ 2 = 1").

68. The **KC** will need to be 14" or longer. If not, choose a long cord from the back to use as the **KC**. Make a tight **R.VHH, L.VHH** around all of the vertical cords. Cut off 2 cords from the back of the bundle. Make a **R.VHH**, cut off 2 cords. Make a **L.VHH**, cut off 2 cords. Make a **R.VHH**, cut off 2 cords. Make a **L.VHH**. There should be 5 vertical cords and 1 **KC** remaining.

69. Pin the band to the board and thread the vertical cords through a soldered ring. Bring the cords to the back and upward. Tie them just above the ring with a piece of spare cord to hole them in place (see Fig. 58).

70. Make a **R.VHH, L.VHH** around the tab, capturing one of the upturned cords (see Fig. 59a), leaving the other upturned cords loose. Repeat until all 5 upturned cords have been captured (see Fig. 60). Remove the spare cord.

71. Continue the chain of **HH**s until they are the desired length (see Fig. 61a). Pass the **KC** through the cords above the ring (see Fig. 61b).

72. Tighten the upturned cords one by one around the ring and **KC**. Carefully cut off the 5 cords flush with the side of the tab (see Fig. 62).

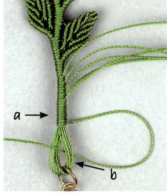
Figure 61

Figure 62

Figure 63

Joan Babcock

Project Thirteen

Figure 64

Figure 65

Figure 66

73. To hide the **KC** within the **HH** chain, first separate the cord into 3 plies (threads). With a sturdy sewing needle, sew each thread (one at a time) upward through the inside of the tab then out to the side, for at least $\frac{1}{4}$" or more (see Fig. 63). Carefully cut off the 3 threads flush with the side of the tab.

Part 5 - Assembling The Sunflower and the Backing

74. Remove one ply from the leftover cord of the center coil and cut it off. Thread the remaining cord onto a narrow embroidery needle. Sew the coil onto the petals (see Fig. 64), making the stitches on the back or in the valleys between the rows of the coil so that they are not visible at the front. Leave the thread attached to use in the next step.

75. Sew the sunflower onto the pendant (Fig. 65) or bracelet (Fig. 66) backing. **Note** - If you are making a pin, sew the pin finding onto the back side of the knotted backing before sewing the sunflower onto the front side of the backing Tie off the thread with a tight **OVK**. Hide the cord end by sewing it between the backing and the sunflower. Cut off the excess cord.

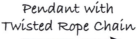

Pendant with Twisted Rope Chain

86 — Margaretenspitze Designs for Jewelry

Sunflower Bracelet

Twisted Rope Pendant Chain

Materials:
Nylon Cords 2 @ 140"
(2) 5mm soldered rings (these are small enough to fit through pendant's 8mm ring)
(1) Clasp

Part 1 - The Chain

1. Thread a 5mm soldered ring onto the 2 cords and position it at the center. Fold the cords in half so that the 4 ends meet up. Pin the ring to your board (see Fig. 1).

2. Beginning Tab - Take one of the cords from the back and make a chain of 11 **HH**s (Half Hitches), starting with a **R.VHH**. The **KC** (Knotting Cord) should exit to the right at the bottom (see Fig. 2).

3. Pattern 1 (dispersing the cords) - The **KC** acts as the 1st lateral cord (see Fig. 3a). Take a cord from the back of the bundle and make a **R.VDHH** around the remaining 2 cords, this is the 2nd lateral cord (see Fig. 3b). Take the cord closest to the back of the bundle and make a **R.VDHH** around the remaining cord (see Fig. 4a). There should be 3 lateral cords and 1 vertical **AC** (Anchor Cord).

4. Pattern 2 (gathering the cords) - Bring the top lateral cord (Fig. 4b) downward vertically. It will be the 1st **AC** in this row (see Fig. 5a). Make a **VDHH** around it with the next lateral cord (see Fig. 5b). Bring the **VDHH** cord downward vertically and join it with the **AC**, so that there are 2 **AC**s. Make a **VDHH** around the 2 **AC**s with the next lateral cord (see Fig. 6a).

5. Bring the **VDHH** cord downward vertically and join it with the 2 **AC**s so that there are 3 **AC**s (see Fig. 7a). Make a **VDHH** around them with the vertical cord on the left (see Fig. 7b).

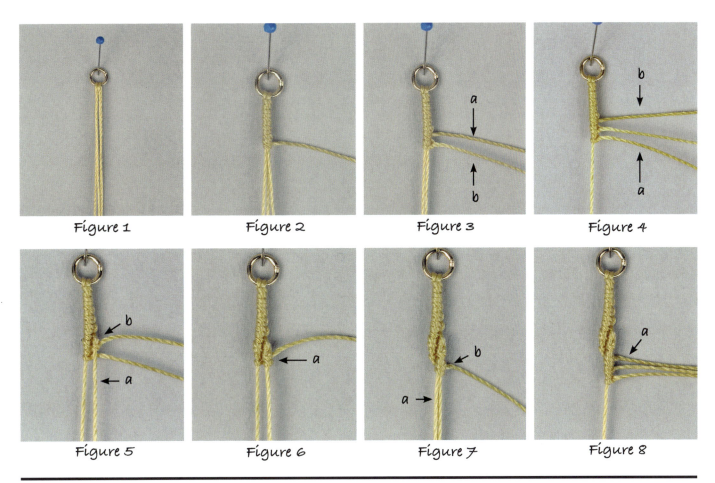

Figure 1   Figure 2   Figure 3   Figure 4
Figure 5   Figure 6   Figure 7   Figure 8

Joan Babcock

Project Thirteen

Figure 9

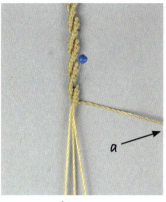
Figure 10

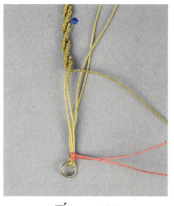
Figure 11

Figure 12

6. Repeat Pattern 1 (Step 3, Figures 2 - 4) **Note -** The cord from the last **VDHH** in Pattern 2 (see Fig. 7b) will also be used as the 1st lateral cord of this pattern (see Fig. 8a).

7. Repeat Pattern 2 (Steps 4 & 5, Figures 5 - 7). Figure 9 shows the completed pattern.

8. Repeat Steps 6 and 7 until the chain is the desired length minus approximately ⅞". Steps 9 - 12 will add an additional ⅞" to the knotted chain. When determining the knotted chain length, factor in the clasp and any additional jump rings that you may use, which will also add to the final length of the chain.

Part 2 - The End Tab & Clasp

9. End Tab - Make an **OVK** (Overhand Knot) at the tip of the lateral cord (see Fig. 10a) to mark it. Repeat Patterns 1 & 2. Cut off the **OVK** cord flush with the bottom of the knotwork. This leaves just 2 **AC**s.

10. Thread a 5mm soldered ring onto the 2 **AC**s and position it about 1" - 1 ½" below the bottom of the chain. Fold the **AC**s towards the back and upwards along side the cords above the ring. Hold them in place by tying a piece of spare cord around all cords just above the ring (see Fig. 11).

11. Make a chain of 11 **HH**s around all the cords (see Fig. 12). **Note -** Relax the tension a little and make this chain slightly looser than usual, which will make the next steps easier.

12. Pull each of the upward cords to reduce the length, leaving about ¼" of space between the bottom of the **HH** chain and the ring. Pass the **KC** through the center of the cords above the jump ring. Continue to pull the cords snugly around the **KC** and the jump ring (see Fig. 13).

13. Untwist the **KC**, separating the 3 plies (see Fig. 13). With a narrow sewing needle, sew each of the threads (one at a time) upward through the inside of the **HH** chain to conceal them (see Fig. 14). Cut them off flush with the knotwork.

14. Cut off the 2 **AC**s flush with the top of the **HH** chain. Thread the Twisted Rope Chain through the ring of the pendant before attaching the clasp parts to the chain (see Fig. 15).

Figure 13

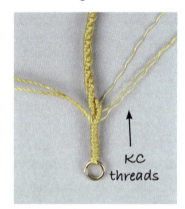
Figure 14

Figure 15

Joan Reeder Babcock

is an internationally recognized fiber artist, jewelry designer, teacher, and author who has been creating one-of-a-kind jewelry and fiber art since 1988.

She is known for her innovative approach which blend cords, beads, and metal elements together. Her unique designs have been featured in numerous fiber art and bead related books and magazines.

She is the author of "Micro-Macramé Jewelry: Tips and Techniques for Knotting with Beads", "Wired Micro-Macramé Jewelry: Enhancing Fiber Designs with Wire", "Micro-Macramé Jewelry ll, Artful Designs for the Adventurous Knotter" and a DVD, "Micro-Macramé & Cavandoli Knotting, Level One".

Joan lives in Santa Fe, New Mexico with her husband and business partner Jeff and their two cats.

You can see her jewelry and fiber art at www.joanbabcock.com and on Facebook at www.facebook.com/Joan-Babcock-Designs.

You can find more of her tutorials, kits, books, and micro-macramé supplies at www.micro-macramejewelry.com.

Printed in Great Britain
by Amazon